DINOSAURS
And Other Prehistoric Animals

Rhamphorhynchus

Pteranodon

Diplodocus

Ornitholestes

INTRODUCTION

Each year, more than two million visitors stream through the halls of The American Museum of Natural History in New York City to marvel at its countless exhibits. Very few of them miss — or, indeed, *want* to miss — famed Dinosaur Hall, where authentic inhabitants millions of years in the past are on display, reconstructed from their very own bones!

Children, especially, are fascinated by our prehistoric specimens, and are anxious to learn all they can about dinosaurs, the creatures who dominated the earth for a longer period than any other animal. In the pages of a book like Darlene Geis's they will find answers to some of the questions formed in their inquisitive young minds as they marvel at *Brontosaurus, Tyrannosaurus* or *Stegosaurus*. They will also find here an introduction to some of the principles of paleontology — the science that deals with all extinct life.

But what of the youngster who does not live near a museum and does not have the opportunity to see for himself the remains of extinct animals? It then becomes our job to bring the "Skeleton Zoos" to him through the pages of a book. For young people this book will prove that truth can be more exciting than legend.

Mary B. Patsuris
Scientific Assistant
Department of Geology and Paleontology
The American Museum of Natural History

DINOSAURS
And Other Prehistoric Animals

Text by Darlene Geis

Pictures by R. F. Peterson

GROSSET & DUNLAP • Publishers • NEW YORK

CONTENTS

STORIES IN STONES

WHEN THE WORLD WAS YOUNG

THE GREAT AGE OF DINOSAURS

THE FINAL AGE OF DINOSAURS

1978 Printing
ISBN: 0-448-02881-6 (Trade Edition)
ISBN: 0-448-03914-1 (Library Edition)

STORIES IN STONES

The Monster of the Badlands

In the folklore of the Sioux Indian tribe, this story has been told around many campfires:

One day, long long years ago, before the white man came to America, a party of Sioux Indian warriors were out hunting. They had left their village far behind. Before they realized it, the group of braves found themselves alone in the bare and rocky badlands of the West.

Suddenly the sky darkened. The broken hills took on a strange color under the stormy clouds. As the braves huddled together, feeling very small in that empty land, a blazing zigzag of lightning ripped the sky. There was a clap of thunder that shook the earth.

Looking up in terror, the Indians thought they saw the shape of a giant bird falling to earth. Less courageous men would have hurried home to their faraway village, thankful for their safety. But these were Sioux Indian braves — and they lived up to their proud name. They went off to find that bird.

The band of hunters traveled over the badlands for days until they came at last to the spot where they thought the giant bird had fallen. Nothing was left of the terrible creature but its bones, and nearby, in some loose rocks, they found a scattering of "thunderstones."

The Indians shuddered as they looked at the monster's skeleton. The bird had fallen so hard, they thought, that its bones were partly sunk in the rock. But the braves could see that its wingspread was as big as four tall men standing on top of one another. The strange creature had fierce claws on its wings, as well as on its feet, and its beak was long and sharp. There was a long, bony crest on its head. The Indians knew that they had never seen a bird like it before.

So the Sioux braves went back to their village with tales of this terrible bird — the thunderbird, as they called it, the mighty spirit who brought the thunder.

9

Truth Is Stranger Than Legend

The thunderbird appears in many Indian tales and Indian art work. Its description is very much like one of the prehistoric flying reptiles that flapped its way through the skies in the days of the dinosaurs.

Had the Indians really seen a prehistoric flying reptile? No, that would have been quite impossible, for the ancient reptiles and dinosaurs had been dead and gone for nearly 70 million years when man's ancestor first swung himself down from the trees.

But the Indians — and many other people in the past — must have come across fossil remains, and thought they were recent. Shells of ancient sea creatures, bodies of ancient fish or land animals, even some plants, have become fossils. But the conditions must have been just right for this to happen.

First, a creature must have been covered, immediately after it had died, with sand or mud or tar or some material that would preserve its bony parts. That material hardened into rock in the course of centuries, and the bones or shells in it were preserved to come down to us as fossils.

People have dug up these rocks with strange shapes and bones in them all through the ages. The name "fossil" comes from a Latin word meaning "to dig up."

Our brave little band of Sioux warriors probably came across the fossil skeleton of a 70-million-year-old flying reptile. But they had no way of knowing how old it was, or even what it was, so they made up a good story to go with it.

The "thunderstones" were fossil shells shaped like small cones. They looked so much like weapons that not only the Indians, but other ancient people as well, thought that they were thunderbolts thrown down from the skies during storms. The real explanation, of course, is that very often, after a bad storm, pieces of rock are washed away and fossils are exposed that were not visible before.

But because no one knew for certain the truth about the huge bones or shapes that they found in the rocks, people had to use their imaginations. And so they made up stories of giants, sea monsters, dragons and, as we have seen, thunderbirds.

We have all heard these stories, but no one has quite believed them. Then, about 150 years ago, a new science began to uncover the truth — a truth that turned out to be stranger than the stories.

There Were Giants in Those Days

And now we know that there really *were* giants in the world long ago! Today we can go to museums and see huge dinosaur skeletons — the bones of animals that once actually walked this earth. And we are struck by how closely some of them resemble the terrible lizard-like dragons of our storybooks. Somehow, seeing the remains of these great beasts before our very eyes, the truth becomes far more marvelous than the fairy tales. And we are eager to find out more about them.

Tall Tales and Superstitions

The ancient Greeks were puzzled by the odd plant and animal shapes they sometimes found in rocks. Some decided that they were a special form of stony life which grew from eggs or seeds sown in the rocks. The Greek historian Herodotus disagreed. He thought that these rock shapes, or fossils, were the remains of ancient creatures which had once lived on this earth. But hardly anyone believed him.

Then, in the Middle Ages, people supposed that the shapes and bones dug up from the rocks had dropped from stars or outer space. They believed them to be a form of star life.

The great 15th century artist and scientist, Leonardo da Vinci, studied his own world carefully, and he came to agree with Herodotus. Fossils were the remains of creatures which had lived on earth when it was very different, long, long ago. But again, hardly anyone wanted to believe that.

Some people believed that these fossil remains must have been creatures drowned in Noah's Flood. But some of the fossil bones were tremendous. How to explain them? Very simply. There were "giant people" before the Flood. A huge skull of a mammoth, with the opening for a trunk in the middle of its forehead, became the skull of the one-eyed giant, Cyclops. Nothing was impossible to explain — but the explanations did not always fit too comfortably.

In 1706 a tooth was dug up near Albany, New York. It weighed two and one-quarter pounds and was nearly six inches long. Governor Dudley of Massachusetts was shown this marvel. (Much later it was found to be a mastodont tooth.) The Governor wrote excitedly about it to Cotton Mather, a noted colonial clergyman and writer, saying that he was certain it was a human tooth — belonging, of course, to a human giant who had died in Noah's Flood. Without doubt, Dudley explained, this giant had waded in the rising waters, his head above the clouds, until at last he, too, was drowned.

However wild and unscientific their guesses were, people were becoming more and more curious about the meaning of fossils. Thomas Jefferson was so interested in fossil remains of animals that he brought his collection with him to the White House when he became President.

Jefferson believed that when the United States was more fully explored, some of the strange creatures would be found, still living in "the immense country to the West and Northwest." He gave instructions to Lewis and Clark, the explorers, to watch for mammoths and giant sloths! Jefferson's guess was off by thousands of years. But the time was ripe now for the discovery of the ancient past.

A New Science Is Born

Just about this time, toward the end of the 18th century, the study of the earth's history became a science instead of a guessing game. From the beginning, the earth has recorded its own history, only no one knew how to read the book. It was all there, written in the rocks, but some of it was worn away, and much of it was disarranged.

The first job was to get the pages in order. A young Englishman named William Smith set out to do this. He was a surveyor who wandered about the English countryside taking measurements. In certain places, where the land was dug away or the side of a hill was exposed, he could see clearly that the rock was laid down in layers.

Over the years, William Smith drew careful diagrams of these layers in different parts of the country. He noticed that certain layers of rock contained fossil shells that were found in no other rock. This, he reasoned, would mean that these layers were formed at the same time, no matter what their location was now. So, in a rough sort of way, he could date some of the layers of rock, and match them up from one part of the country to the other.

These layers of rock were formed from the sand or mud or shells that were deposited by water, and thousands of years later, hardened into rock. They were called strata. And Smith was nicknamed "Strata" Smith because of his lifelong interest in mapping and dating the rock layers. Later scientists were greatly indebted to "Strata" Smith. He had made a start in setting the earth's pages in order, and also in indicating on which pages certain fossil facts could be found.

The scientists who studied the history of the earth from its rocks were called geologists (jee-OL-uh-jists). The new scientists who studied the history of ancient life on earth from the fossils in the rocks were called paleontologists (pale-ee-on-TOL-uh-jists). Together, the two groups tried to put the pages of earth history in order, and then read the meaning of what was written on them in fossil remains.

But the scientists often received their most valuable help from outsiders. One of these outsiders was a twelve-year-old girl named Mary Anning.

The Girl Who Found a Dragon

Mary Anning lived in the English seacoast village of Lyme Regis. From the time she was five years old, her father used to take her with him to hunt fossil shells on the cliffs and beaches outside the town. Then he sold the fossils as "curiosities" to the summer visitors who came to enjoy the bathing and the fresh sea air.

When Mary was ten her father died. But she carried on the difficult and dangerous work herself. In fact, the little girl was quite an expert.

Then one day in 1811, when she was only twelve years old, Mary Anning made one of the great discoveries of her time. She found her first "dragon." It was a skeleton of fossil bones imbedded in a blue slate layer of the cliff. There it lay, almost seven feet long, later described as a creature with the snout of a dolphin, the teeth of a crocodile, the skull and chest of a lizard, the paddles of a whale, and the vertebrae (or backbone) of a fish.

Some men from the village helped Mary pry the heavy stone loose from the cliff. She realized at once that her dragon was no mere curiosity for summer visitors. So she had it taken to the lord of the manor who paid her more than a hundred dollars for it.

He sent it to a museum, and scientists from all over the world studied the fossil dragon. Since it seemed to be half fish and half lizard, they combined the Greek words for fish and lizard into the name ichthyosaur (IK-thee-uh-sor).

Mary Anning collected specimens for scientists from then on. She learned about the different rock layers in the cliffs, and which ones might hold the fossils she wanted. Later, she found the fossil of a kind of ancient sea serpent called a plesiosaur (PLEES-ee-uh-sor). Some years after, Mary made her third great discovery. It was the skeleton of a flying reptile called a pterosaur (TER-uh-sor), and it was the first to be found in Britain.

We will meet all of her dragons later in their proper places. But this is the place for Mary's story. Scientists all over the world knew her work and were grateful for her fossils. She even had a king for a customer. The King of Saxony visited her shop and bought an ichthyosaur fossil from her. When Mary Anning died, a stained glass window was put in the Lyme Regis church in her memory.

The Men Who Read the Stones

The men who were pioneers in that unknown world of the ancient past had to be part detective and part explorer. Some clues were brought to them by people like Mary Anning, or workmen in quarries and mines who unearthed strange fossils.

But the new science could not be studied in a laboratory alone. These scientists had to put on sturdy boots and learn how to handle tools. In order to discover the past, they had to get out and explore at first hand the rocky and difficult country where history was recorded.

One of the early British geologists, Dr. James Hutton, found the key to reading the earth's past in its rocks. "The past history of our globe," he pointed out simply, "must be explained by what can be seen to be happening now." So we learned that the rivers and seas, the wind and rain and frost changed the surface of the earth in the past, even as it happens today.

The French naturalist, Baron Georges Cuvier, was the first man to make a careful study of backboned animals (vertebrates) and especially the fossil vertebrates. It was he who described Mary Anning's dragon so well. He first pointed out the similarities and differences that exist between many kinds of skeletons. As a result of his work, it was now impossible for a scientist to confuse the tooth of a mastodon with that of a human, as Governor Dudley had done.

Dr. Gideon Mantell was a physician whose hobby was digging up and studying fossils. After he found the teeth and some bones of the first dinosaur discovered in England, Mantell spent a great deal of time digging for fossils, and writing some of the first scientific papers on the subject.

In America, in the first half of the 19th century, Edward Hitchcock, a professor at Amherst College, tried to solve the mystery of the giant three-toed footprints found in some Connecticut rocks. Since very little was known about dinosaurs then, Hitchcock misread his rocks and thought they were great bird tracks.

The man who really gave the study of fossil animals its start in the United States was Dr. Joseph Leidy. The first dinosaur dug up in this country was a loose collection of odd bones from an excavation in a suburb of Philadelphia. Leidy worked on fitting them together, but many were missing. So part of his task was to go around the countryside trying to buy up the missing dinosaur parts being used as bric-a-brac and doorstops by New Jersey housewives. The dinosaur turned out to be one of the so-called duck-billed dinosaurs whom you will meet later in this book, or you may see him "in person" at the Philadelphia Academy of Natural Sciences.

The work of the next two great American paleontologists brings us close to the 20th century. Othniel Charles Marsh and Edward Drinker Cope put the new science on an entirely new basis. Instead of waiting for a lucky accident to turn up some fossil bones, they organized expeditions as carefully as big game hunters.

Thomas Jefferson had been correct when he said that once we explored the West we would find some strange animals there. Geologic surveys, which were set up to find out about the natural resources of the new land, also disclosed some marvelous fossil beds out West. And it was there that Professors Marsh and Cope found their happy hunting grounds for the strange animals which had been dead for millions of years.

Marsh, whose enormous fossil and dinosaur collection is at the Peabody Museum at Yale University, hired Buffalo Bill, the famous scout and Indian fighter, to guide him through the Western badlands.

Cope, whose great collection now belongs to the American Museum of Natural History in New York City, was always competing with Marsh. The two professors fought over the dinosaur fossils as jealously as a couple of dogs over bones. But in the end the winner in this fight was the new science.

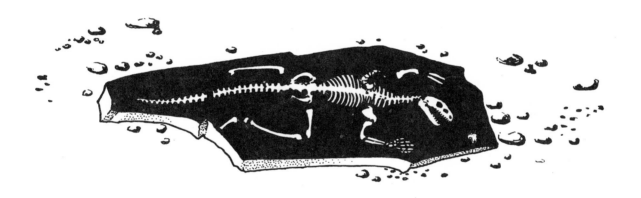

Back to the Beginning

By the early part of the 20th century, much of the story of the earth and its inhabitants had been learned from the rocks. There are still gaps and questions and unexplored territory. But perhaps some of you boys and girls who are reading this now will grow up to write the new pages in the earth's story. It is all waiting for you in the patient stones.

But now we are going back to the beginning of the world. You will see, chapter by chapter, the amazing story that has come from those stones as a result of the scientists' study and hard work. And you will see some of the big question marks that still remain — perhaps for you to answer.

WHEN THE WORLD WAS YOUNG

In the Beginning

Right at the start there is a big question that is still unanswered. Just exactly how was the earth formed? No one knows for sure. But scientists believe that originally it was a spinning ball of white-hot stardust and gases which finally thickened into a ball of red-hot liquid as it cooled. Cooling still more, the earth developed a solid crust of rock, while heavier molten metals sank to the center of the ball.

This rock crust was made of granite and basalt, and it was fiercely hot. For a long, long time, rain fell and sizzled into steam as it touched the rock. But finally, as the crust grew cooler, the rain collected into steaming pools and lakes, and trickled down the rocks in little rivers.

Great islands of granite rock that were lighter than the molten metal inside the sphere rose up and formed the first blocks of continents. As the rain washed over these rocky continents and ran down in rivers to the sea, it carried bits of rocky sediment with it. These bits of rocky sediment sank to the bottom of the water and after thousands of years they hardened into new layers of rock.

The Calendar of Earth History

Geologists can see the rain and rivers washing rock and land into the sea now. That is their clue to what must have happened in the past. And judging from how many layers of rock sediment there are, and how long it takes them to form, they have estimated the earth's age to be about three billion years.

We can now measure the rate of radioactive change in rocks, and date them that way, too. The rocks are their own calendar. Of course, as "Strata" Smith found, rock layers are not neatly arranged any more. If they were, they would have reached a thickness on the earth's surface of 95 miles. Instead, as the earth continued to cool, it shrank. The crust of rock wrinkled and folded and cracked like the skin of a dried prune.

Thus, many of the layers were pushed up into mountains, which were then worn away by wind and rain and frost, and lost forever. And volcanoes erupted and sent jets of molten rock into the layers of sedimentary rock, so the original order is not always easy to figure out.

But geologists have seen that the history of the earth had at least three ages of great mountain-making activity. These show in the rock layers, and divide

THE CALENDAR OF EARTH HISTORY

The Record of Life on Earth as Told in its Rocks

ERAS	PERIODS	RULING ANIMALS
CENOZOIC (Recent Life) 70 Million Years	Quaternary	Man
	Tertiary	Mammals
MESOZOIC (Middle Life) 130 Million Years	Cretaceous	Dinosaurs
	Jurassic	
	Triassic	
PALEOZOIC (Ancient Life) 300 Million Years	Permian	Early Reptiles
	Carboniferous	
	Devonian	Amphibians
	Silurian	Fish
	Ordovician	Invertebrates
	Cambrian	
PROTEROZOIC (Former Life) **ARCHEOZOIC** (Beginning Life) 2,500 Million Years	Pre-Cambrian	Earliest Life No Fossil Remains

the earth's history into four large chapters. Each chapter tells a similar story — the continents rise, mountain ranges are pushed up, volcanoes erupt. The seas become smaller and deeper, and the climate becomes extreme. Then there is a long period when the mountains are worn down, the land is flooded, sediment is deposited on the floor of the shallow seas, the climate is milder. Then a new chapter is ready to begin all over again.

Scientists have made an orderly chart of the earth's history based upon these changes in the rock layers which they have studied. The history is divided into large chapters, or eras, and within them are smaller periods.

The eras and periods are all marked by the occurrence of great changes in the earth's surface. And those changes resulted in changing forms of life as life fitted itself to the new conditions.

The names of these eras and periods are the same all over the world. The eras were given names from Greek words — Cenozoic (see-nuh-ZOH-ik) or Recent Life, Mesozoic (MESS-uh-zoh-ik) or Middle Life, and Paleozoic (PALE-ee-uh zoh-ik) or Ancient Life.

The periods were named by the scientists who first studied their story in certain rock layers. The scientists named the period after the rock layers, or the place where they studied them.

For example, the Triassic (try-ASS-ik) period comes from a word meaning "group of three." That was because the scientist who first studied the rocks of this period in Germany found them to be laid down in triple layers.

The Jurassic (joo-RASS-ik) period was named for the Jura Mountains where those layers were first studied. And the Cretaceous (kree-TAY-shuss) period was so named because in some parts of the world its rock layers were very chalky — Cretaceous comes from the Latin word for chalk.

Wherever in the world the rock layers of these periods are now found they are called by the name of the period. So there is Jurassic rock in America, far from the Jura Mountains. And Triassic rock is rock that dates from that period, whether it is formed in triple layers or not.

These names, used everywhere in the world, are a great convenience to people studying the earth's history. We can look at a chart and see the chapters all in order and read the history of our planet. And it is a history that is the same for all peoples of all countries, even in its language.

Our story begins at the bottom of the Calendar of Earth History. Not much is known of those times, when there was nothing living to leave its record in the rocks. Even the earliest forms of life had no hard parts to be preserved or to leave imprints for the ages. But scientists have made some educated guesses about what the world was like two and one-half billion years ago.

Life at Last

For a long, long time, the earth must have looked somewhat like the moon. It was a dreary place of bare rock, wild mountains, rivers and seas. Every so often, the dreadful rumble of volcanoes and their fiery light would disturb the landscape.

Then, about two and one-half billion years ago, tiny specks of living matter appeared in the warm seas. No one knows yet how such life began. It might have been from the combination of sunlight and certain chemicals in the warm shallow waters. But from this first life that was neither animal nor plant, the first tiny animal and plant life developed in the seas.

The Watery World

As time rolled on and millions of years passed, sea plants and sea animals with hard shells filled the waters that nearly covered the earth. When they died, their shells dropped to the bottom of the sea. Sand and mud covered them, and in the course of thousands of years the sand hardened into rock.

Many of the shells left their outlines in the hard rock. So although the shell itself is no longer there, a perfect print of it is left in stone. This is a shell fossil, and so many of these sea shell fossils have been found all over the world that we can tell where the early oceans must have been.

There was still no life on the land, not a blade of grass or any growing thing, but the oceans were teeming with life. Some shellfish grew to be 15 feet long. The creatures all had soft insides with hard spines or shells on the outside. They were called invertebrates, which means "without backbones."

Finally the first fishes swam into the watery world. The age of the vertebrates, or backboned animals, was born. And that is the age we live in today. We, and many of the animals, both ancient and modern, are vertebrates. We all have skeletons with backbones. These early fishes, then, were the ancestors of all the backboned animals that developed later.

Land Alive!

About 325 million years ago another great change took place. The land masses rose up higher out of the water, and the oceans became smaller. Nothing grew on the bare rocky land. But as oceans and rivers shrank and dried up around the edges, some plants were stranded on the muddy shores.

Some of these plants were able to live out of water. They multiplied and spread. The others died. Through 50 million long years, the land plants changed, grew roots and branches and seeds. They spread from the marshy shores inland. And then the bare rocks were clothed in green and there was food on the land. Scorpions and snails were the first air-breathing animals to come up onto the shores and eat the land plants. The first insects followed the plant life onto land and they have continued to develop to this day.

After the continents had risen and the seas had shrunk and the volcanoes had erupted violently, there came a great change in climate. The warm, moist climate that had been so good for plants — almost like a hothouse — became very dry. There were drenching rains for a short period, and again came the dryness.

As a result, lakes and rivers would be in high flood for a few months. Then they would dry up suddenly when the rainy season was over. This meant that many creatures were stranded — really stuck in the mud — when this happened. Many of the shallow-water fish flopped and floundered helplessly as the water dried away beneath them, and they died.

The lungfishes were one type of fish that was able to survive during the dry periods. We can see their descendants to this day in parts of Africa, Australia, and South America, where the rivers are in flood at one season and nearly dry the next. The lungfish can take in some oxygen out of the air, and stay inactive, almost in hibernation, during the dry times when it is impossible for it to swim and live like a fish.

The lobefins were another group of fish who were able to change with the times to survive. Coelacanths (SEE-luh-kanths) were lobefins. People thought that coelacanths had died out 60 million years ago. Imagine the excitement, then, when a live one was brought up in a fisherman's net off the coast of Africa in 1938! It was such a queer-looking fish that someone took it to the museum. But there it was skinned and stuffed, as dead fish spoil quickly, especially in the African heat. By the time an expert was able to get to the museum, there was only the coelacanth's skin left to study. The disappointed scientist had to wait fourteen more years before another coelacanth turned up. This time it was kept on ice for him, and he was finally able to study his living fossil inside and out.

Coelacanth

The First Footprints

The lobefins were able to change through the years and adapt to this wet and dry kind of life in their own way. They had an air-filled sac inside them, which helped them float and balance more easily in the water. They also had two pairs of rounded fins with a bony skeleton. These four bony fins were the forerunners of the primitive amphibian leg.

When the lakes and rivers dried up it was the lobefins who first refused to be stick-in-the-muds. Perhaps, at the beginning, some of them were freaks who could take oxygen out of the air directly into their lungs.

Perhaps a few stronger ones, who wanted desperately to live, managed to flop out of the mud on their four fins and cross the land to a deeper pond. At any rate, it was these air-breathing fin-walkers who survived and produced their young. And their young grew better suited to moving on land with each generation.

Finally, the fins became legs and feet and the first land animals crawled in the muddy marshland near the water. We have found their footprints in the rocks. These first creatures to crawl up on land were called amphibians (am-FIB-ee-uns), from the Greek words meaning "leading a double life." They laid their eggs in the water, and the young lived in the water. But upon maturing, they moved up on land and were able to breathe and feed there.

Frogs, toads and salamanders are modern amphibians. The early amphibians were very fishlike. They had heavy bones and thick bodies like their fishy ancestors. But since they did not have the help of water to support them, they moved slowly and awkwardly on land. Their limbs stuck out sideways from their bodies, keeping them close to the ground.

The first land creatures looked like crawling fish — much more at home in the water that they were leaving than on the land that they were about to conquer.

Diplocaulus

Diplocaulus (dip-luh-KAWL-us)

One of the oddest little creatures on land or sea was the early amphibian called *Diplocaulus*. His name means "double shaft" or "stalk" which describes the way his vertebrae were formed. This amphibian lived on the muddy bottom of the shallow water near the shore. Because he never developed the ability to breathe with lungs as land animals do, this amphibian spent most of his life in the water.

Diplocaulus was about two feet long, and he had a broad flat body and skull. His large head formed a triangular shape with two winglike points sticking far out at each side, and this unusual shape was his most distinctive feature. His legs were small and weak, but in swimming, *Diplocaulus* found his tail much more useful. He was an experiment that turned out not to be successful, and his kind died out.

But there were other amphibians who were better suited to a life on land. They developed strong backbones and powerful legs, and for a while they were the rulers of the world.

Eryops

Eryops (ER-ee-ops)

The largest and most savage of the amphibians was a creature who outwardly resembled a crocodile. His name was *Eryops,* which means "drawn-out face," and his fossil remains have been found in Texas. Some of them were nine feet long.

The skull and skeleton of *Eryops* are well known to paleontologists and, interestingly enough, he is one of the few prehistoric amphibians whose skin is also known. At first, scientists wondered if this animal had been smooth- or pebbly-skinned. Then, a "mummified" specimen of *Eryops* was discovered in Texas. Scientists made a careful examination of the rock which surrounded their specimen and found that it contained impressions of the animal's skin. It was also found, after further investigation, that *Eryops'* skin had been composed of small, flat, bony plates embedded in leathery skin. This unusual specimen may be seen in the collections of Harvard University in Cambridge, Massachusetts.

Eryops had a large mouth with wicked-looking teeth, and he was carnivorous, which means that he fed on meat rather than on plants. His legs were powerful, but short, and they grew out of his body from his sides which made him clumsy and slow. He also had a long, heavy tail to drag after him, which was quite useless.

But *Eryops'* big disadvantage was that the eggs of his young had to be laid in water. They had a soft covering, like fish eggs, instead of a shell. So the young first grew up in water, and later came out on land to live. This meant that these big hungry creatures could never be too far away from the water in which they had to lay their eggs.

When new changes in the world dried up the inland waters and the swamps, and the climate became colder, the land was no longer so friendly a place for amphibians. Eventually many kinds of amphibians died out completely.

Seymouria (see-MOOR-ee-uh)

As the world changed and became drier and colder the amphibians found it more and more difficult to get along. There were fewer places where they could lay their soft-shelled eggs in water. And with their spraddle legs sticking out sideways they could certainly not travel long distances over the land to get to suitable egg-laying places.

Finally, however, one kind of amphibian was able to lay its eggs on land. This was probably a small creature, not very exciting when compared with the great *Eryops*. But once the climate had changed, and the world had become drier, this little fellow was far better off than *Eryops* and the other amphibians. He was the ancestor of all the great reptiles that were to follow.

Among the red rocks of Texas, scientists dug up the fossil of a lizard-like creature about two and one-half feet long. It was an important discovery, and the scientists named it *Seymouria,* after the nearby town of Seymour in northern Texas.

Seymouria is important because he is a kind of missing link between amphibians and reptiles. It is hard to say whether *Seymouria* was an amphibian who was about to become a reptile, or a reptile that had just stopped being an amphibian. Scientists do not agree on this.

He had the broad, flat head, widespread legs and tadpole tail of his amphibian ancestors. But he also had certain reptile characteristics, for his backbone was like that of a reptile. So he is the bridge between the two groups, amphibians and reptiles.

No one knows for sure what kind of egg *Seymouria* laid, nor where. Was it an egg with a soft covering laid in water, or was it a hard-shelled egg laid on land? Until paleontologists learn the answers to these questions, they will not be able to determine if *Seymouria* was really an amphibian or a reptile. If *Seymouria* laid its eggs in the water, then this prehistoric animal would be classified as an amphibian. But if *Seymouria* laid its eggs on land, science would identify the "missing link" as a reptile.

Seymouria

The Reptiles Take Over

While the giant *Eryops* was still king of the land, some of his smaller subjects were creeping around who would one day rule instead. These little creatures were originally amphibians too, and they still looked much like them. They were called reptiles, which means "those who creep."

But reptiles had developed the remarkable ability to lay their eggs on land. And when their young hatched out of the egg, they were land animals from their first breath and their first step. Now, if the world had not become drier, this might not have been such an important advantage for the reptiles. But as things turned out, amphibians were soon on the way out and the reptiles took over.

The hard-shelled reptile egg had pores which let air through. It had moisture and nourishing food — the yolk — for the new life within it. When that life hatched, it was a fully formed land animal. Furthermore, since it only had to be fit to lead one kind of life, it could improve itself for life on land. Its skeleton, its muscles, even its brain, were finally an improvement over the amphibians'.

The reptiles ruled the world for nearly 150 million years, which indicates that they were a very successful form of life. They branched out into hundreds of forms, including dinosaurs, which were the largest land animals ever to live. And we must remember, too, that the mammals who rule the animal kingdom today are descended from reptiles.

Edaphosaurus (ee-daf-uh-SOR-us)

The red sandstone of Texas was also the resting place for the fossils of this early reptile. *Edaphosaurus* means "foundation" or "base lizard," and he was probably called this because he was shaped like a long-tailed lizard. But because of the odd sail on his back he looked like a full-rigged ship.

Edaphosaurus lived along the shores of streams or lakes, and he ate the plants that grew there. His head was small, and he had small teeth around the edges of his jaws, and rows of crushing teeth on his palate — all very useful for grinding up his vegetarian diet and getting the juice from the plants.

Edaphosaurus

Dimetrodon (dye-MET-ruh-don)

Dimetrodon means "double-measure tooth" and this name was given to him because the reptile had two different sizes of teeth in his jaws. *Dimetrodon* was found in the same place as *Edaphosaurus*, and he, too, carried a large curving "sail" on his back. But by one look at his head, you will see that this was a reptile of a different diet. *Dimetrodon* had a large skull and jaws, and his teeth were dagger points and sharp as knife blades. He skipped the vegetables and concentrated on raw meat. And his favorite meat was that other sail-bearing fellow, his cousin, *Edaphosaurus!*

Scientists are not certain about the purpose of the strange sail on his back. Their best guess is that it was a natural air conditioner that regulated the animal's temperature in some way — or perhaps it was just a fancy-looking nuisance!

Dimetrodon

Cynognathus

Cynognathus (sine-og-NATH-us)

Cynognathus means "dog-jawed reptile." He got his name because his jaws and teeth were doglike.

The reptiles were developing into creatures better suited to getting around on land. Their legs were lengthening, and instead of sprawling out from the animals' sides they supported the body from underneath. This enabled the animal to be more active.

Cynognathus was a reptile who was becoming more like a mammal. He was about four or five feet long, and very active. Activity is a characteristic of warm-blooded animals. Cold-blooded reptiles can even stop breathing for a time, and still be alive. But mammals cannot. So perhaps this active meat-eating *Cynognathus* was beginning to be warm-blooded. Scientists are not certain.

But they do know that *Cynognathus* had the kind of teeth found later in mammals — the canines, or long dagger-shaped teeth, the incisors for biting, and the molars for grinding and chewing. And that makes him the structural ancestor of the mammals, which is the reason scientists study his fossil remains with great interest.

The Dinosaurs' Little Grandfather

There were many strange and wonderful reptiles living at this time. Some of them looked like nightmare monsters. Some had enormous heads. Some were large and fierce. But there was one group of small, not very special-looking reptiles that turned out to be the most important of all. They were important because they were the ancestors of the great dinosaurs, of modern crocodiles, and of the first flying reptiles.

These small lizard-like creatures developed strong hind legs on which they ran or stood. They had long and powerful tails which helped support and balance them in their upright position. And their front legs were tiny and were carried close to the chest, like little arms.

Saltoposuchus

Saltoposuchus (sal-tuh-puh-SOOK-us)

The grandfather of the tremendous and magnificent dinosaurs was a little hurrying, scurrying creature who ran along the ground on his hind legs. His name was *Saltoposuchus.*

This little meat-eating reptile was not quite four feet long from the tip of his slender tail to the front of his narrow sharp-toothed snout. His small clawlike front legs were like hands for grasping and tearing his prey.

Saltoposuchus leaned slightly forward, with his long tail helping him to balance on his hind legs. His little forelegs were too short and weak to use for running, but this turned out to be a great advantage. Being light and slender, *Saltoposuchus* was swift enough when chasing his prey on two legs. And then he still had two arms with which to snatch at the creatures he was hunting — an improvement over anything that four-legged hunters could do.

Though this reptile was small, he was fierce for his size, and was the terror of all the small creatures on whom he fed. All the dinosaurs were descended from him, and the very earliest ones were probably small, meat-eating creatures who ran about on their hind legs, as he did.

It was only when the dinosaurs grew too large to support their weight on two legs that they dropped down to all fours. Then their hunting days were over, and they became gentle plant-eaters. But those who·continued to walk on their hind legs continued to live on a meat diet. They were the fierce hunters who pursued *Saltoposuchus.*

Looking at his picture, it is difficult for us to see a family resemblance between *Saltoposuchus* and his mighty grandchildren, the dinosaurs. But paleontologists see in this little fellow's bone structure a miniature blueprint of the mighty creatures who were to rule the world for so long.

A new and more powerful kind of hip structure had to develop because of the animal's more upright posture. It is almost identical with the three-branched structure seen in the skeletons of the first great dinosaurs. Also, there were two openings in the skull, one in front of each eye, and this made it possible for even a huge skull to be light in weight, though still strong.

So, hats off to little *Saltoposuchus,* whose descendants would improve on his basic pattern and rule the world for 100 million years!

THE GREAT AGE OF DINOSAURS

200 Million Years Ago

The early reptiles had appeared on the land when the great amphibians, like *Eryops*, still ruled it. But the changes on the earth's surface that were to introduce a new era were taking place. The Era of Ancient Life (Paleozoic) was about to give way to the Era of Middle Life (Mesozoic). The warm moist climate, the swamps and marshes and lush green plants that were ideal for amphibians, were disappearing.

The earth's surface heaved and twisted. There was to be another great change of scene, another new chapter in earth's history. Those forms of life that could change to get along in a new kind of world would live to play a part in the new chapter. The rest were finished.

New mountain ranges were pushed up. The waters that had covered the land were forced back into smaller, deeper seas. Swamps drained dry, and the ferns and swamp trees were replaced in large areas by newer plant life — the ancestors of our firs and pine trees and palms. The Petrified Forest of Arizona was made up of some of these trees.

The reptiles who could roam over a drier, colder, less friendly land survived. The first small mammals appeared on the scene, but many millions of years would have to pass before they became important.

As the climate warmed up again, little *Saltoposuchus* and other small reptiles increased. They branched out into different reptile families, but the chief family of the next 100 million years was the dinosaurs.

Brontosaurus

How Dinosaurs Got the Wrong Name

When the first giant bones of ancient animals were dug up in the 19th century, people became very excited about them. Not much was known of these monsters at the time. Sir Richard Owen, the great British paleontologist, was making a study of the huge fossil remains of these lizard-like reptiles, and he invented a name that he thought would do for the entire group. He took the Greek words for "terrible" and "lizard" and put them together into "dinosaur."

Certainly the description was a good one for the monstrous creatures that had been dug up and assembled at that time. But later scientists discovered that prehistoric reptiles came in assorted sizes, and some of them were small and not at all terrible.

And as more and different kinds of dinosaurs were dug up, a study of their skeletons showed that they could be divided into two quite separate groups. Nevertheless, "dinosaur" was a convenient name to use, and we use it today to include both groups of the prehistoric reptiles.

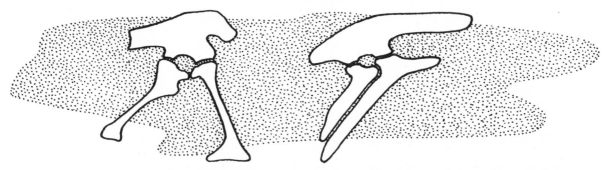

"Lizard-hipped" Saurischian pelvis   *"Bird-hipped" Ornithiscian pelvis*

The Two Kinds of Dinosaurs

The great-great grandchildren of the two-legged *Saltoposuchus* were like him in several ways. At first, they all walked on their hind legs, they were small, and many of them liked the same diet — meat.

But even these first dinosaurs were divided into two groups. Because the hip structure in their skeletons was so different, one group was called lizard-hipped; the other bird-hipped. The lizard-hipped dinosaurs were built more like *Saltoposuchus*. The bird-hipped dinosaurs were more advanced.

The lizard-hipped dinosaurs were originally all meat-eaters. And, in fact, the fierce meat-eating dinosaurs that followed in time came only from this group.

The bird-hipped dinosaurs developed later, and were plant-eaters from the very first. They were a more highly developed form of dinosaur, and they were the last of the dinosaurs to die out.

The Dinosaur Giants

The Mesozoic Era (the Era of Middle Life) lasted about 120 million years. It was divided into three great periods — the Triassic, Jurassic and Cretaceous. During the Triassic period there were more dinosaurs than all the other reptiles in the world. But they had not yet grown to be the size of some of the monsters we see in museums today.

It was during the 35 million years of the Jurassic period that dinosaurs grew great. The climate was just right for them. It had become warm and moist again, and cold-blooded reptiles could live comfortably in the tropical world.

The great plains were jungle, densely covered with lush green plants. Shallow pools and lakes and marshes were dotted with greenery. The dinosaurs browsed and munched and strode across the land, kings of all they surveyed.

The lizard-hipped dinosaurs grew huge, and when their size increased, two things happened. Many of them were no longer quick enough to catch other animals for food. So they became plant-eaters. And the bigger they became, the harder it was to walk on two legs, so most of the lizard-hipped vegetarians dropped down on all fours. Even then, it wasn't easy to lug 40 tons around!

If you look closely at dinosaur skeletons, you will see that their front legs are shorter than their hind legs, and this gives them a clumsy high-hipped look.

The few lizard-hipped dinosaurs who continued to prefer a raw meat diet never grew as large as their vegetarian cousins. But they were a lot quicker as they ran on their two big hind legs — and a lot fiercer!

There are always more plant-eating animals in a community than there are meat-eating animals. If that were not the case, the community would soon eat itself up. And this was true when the dinosaurs ruled the world. There were many sluggish giants who spent their time in the marshes chomping on plants. There were other peaceable monsters who clumped up on land, protected by fierce-looking armor. They too ate plants. And there were some small vegetarian dinosaurs scurrying around in the underbrush. But in animal communities there must always be the beasts of prey, the hunters who live on peaceful creatures. It is one of the harsh rules of the balance of Nature.

In the dinosaur's world, there was a ferocious meat-eater who hunted the large vegetarians. And there was a small dinosaur who preyed on the smaller animals. But the balance was right, for they all lived side by side for millions of years.

When you consider that man has been on this earth for only one million years, you will have some idea of how long and how successfully the dinosaurs ruled.

Why the Difficult Names?

We are about to be introduced to some of the great dinosaurs, and any proper introduction is made by giving the name. Now, dinosaurs themselves are not only large and strange — they bear large and strange names, too. But if you understand how and why they were named, it will seem quite simple, and you will soon be rattling off *Allosaurus* as easily as you can say "hippopotamus."

Scientists are always trying to bring order into the world. We saw how "Strata" Smith put the layers of rock into proper order, for example. Scientists have made the plant and animal kingdoms more orderly, too, by giving names — scientific names — to every living thing in the world. These names are usually made up from Latin or Greek words. Once a thing is named, that name is used for it in all countries, for all time.

In a way, a scientific name is really simpler to learn, since you will never have to relearn it in French, or German, or Russian or Spanish. People everywhere will call an *Allosaurus* an *Allosaurus,* you can be sure.

Each time you come across a new name in this book, remember that it is not just an alphabet jumble, however long it looks. It will be made up from two or three Latin or Greek words that mean something describing the animal, and the English meaning will be explained.

Now step right up and meet the dinosaurs. To name them is to know them.

Allosaurus

Allosaurus (al-uh-SOR-us)

Allosaurus' name comes from the Greek words meaning "other lizard." It is a rather tame name for a fierce beast.

The world at this time would have been a dinosaur paradise if it weren't for the terrible *Allosaurus*. It was as though everything had been granted the dinosaurs for a good life, and then this terror was let loose to disturb the peace.

Allosaurus was a terror, indeed — almost 35 feet long, with powerful hind legs for running down his prey, and dagger-toothed jaws for finishing off the big game he hunted. He had a long tail for balance. The forelegs of this beast were small. But look closely, and you will see that each hand had three heavy curved claws, like meathooks, for tearing and holding his food.

Although *Allosaurus* had a large head, it was designed more as a weapon of destruction than as a brain case. These meat-eating dinosaurs probably did not stalk their game, the big, dull-witted fellows who munched plants, and so the hunt was nothing that needed cunning or cleverness. It was simply a case of teeth and claws against tons and tail. There were only two kinds of defense against teeth and claws. One was for a dinosaur to go out some distance into the water and stay there, safe from *Allosaurus'* hungry jaws. The other was to grow protective armor over a body that was otherwise an unprotected target, and hope for the best.

Some dinosaurs did one, some the other, but the fact remains that both *Allosaurus* and the dinosaurs on which he fed ranged over the world for 35 million years. So each must have been partly successful.

40

Brontosaurus (bron-tuh-SOR-us)

Brontosaurus means "thunder lizard." The scientist who named him must have imagined how the ground shook and thundered each time the *Brontosaurus* took a heavy step with his tree-trunk legs.

Fossil skeletons of *Brontosaurus* have been found in North America. When the scientists put the first one together, they might well have thought there had been a mistake made somewhere!

Imagine an animal measuring 70 feet long, with a heavy tail that went on and on, finally tapering to a long thin point. Imagine a blimp-sized body, supported on four tree-trunk legs, with a neck almost as long as its tail. And for the final ridiculous touch, imagine a tiny head no bigger around than the neck, with a small mouth and a few dozen weak, peg-shaped teeth.

As it turned out, that is just what *Brontosaurus* looked like. And this odd-looking animal was evidently suited to his kind of life. He spent a great deal of time in the shallow water, which helped support his 30-ton weight! To be sure, the water was also his best means of protection against the meat-eating land animals. The tender juicy water plants were his favorite food.

And when his dreaded enemy, *Allosaurus,* came in sight, he could move out into deeper water and still keep his head on its long neck well above the surface. He did not even have to stop eating. In fact, *Brontosaurus* could even munch on his plants under water, so long as he came up for air at intervals.

Sometimes *Brontosaurus* was not so lucky. Sometimes he was caught on the land not far from the water's edge. Then all he could do was turn tail and move as fast as his size permitted to the safety of the lake. Maybe his long tail came in handy then to use as a whiplash against the enemy who was pursuing him.

At the American Museum of Natural History in New York you can see the record of just such a chase as it was written in the mud (which is now rock) 120 million years ago. There are the big basin-shaped footprints of *Brontosaurus,* each with three deep claw-marks to keep him from slipping in the mud. And further back, in among the larger footprints are the three-pronged, birdlike prints of *Allosaurus.*

Did he catch *Brontosaurus* and eat him on the spot? Or did the big peaceful fellow get into the water in the nick of time? We will never know.

Brontosaurus had a tiny brain which probably could not do much more than warn him of danger, tell him where food was and work his jaws. At the base of his backbone, there was a swelling several times larger than his brain. This was a second nerve center, or a second "brain."

Brachiosaurus (brak-ee-uh-SOR-us)

The Greek words meaning "arm lizard" give this giant among giants his name. The bones of his forearm were very large, and his name refers to them.

Brachiosaurus lived in North America and also in East Africa. He probably weighed close to 50 tons, the heaviest of all the dinosaurs.

In *Brachiosaurus* you can see how wasteful and useless great size could be. Here was an animal so heavy that he was barely able to move around on land. As a result, he could neither fight nor run away from his enemies who were much smaller.

This tremendous dinosaur, the biggest of them all, was forced to spend most of his life standing in deep water. Since he couldn't swim either, this must have been a dull way to live — even for a dinosaur!

There are several clues in his body structure that tell scientists how this creature lived. His front legs were much longer than his back ones, which is an unusual characteristic in dinosaurs. Then, his neck extended above his shoulders so high that he could have looked over a three-story building. And to top it off, he had nostrils raised up in a little dome at the top of his head.

Because of these features, scientists think that *Brachiosaurus* spent a good deal of time in very deep water where he could be completely submerged except for the breathing dome that crowned his head. The fact that his body and legs were so heavy probably made it easier for him to have steady footing in deep water. Again, it is the same principle as a deep-sea diver's weighted suit.

All the big, slow, wading dinosaurs were probably the first to die out. They needed low marshy lands and the kind of soft plants that grew there. Toward the end of the Mesozoic Era, when the land began to rise again and the swamps to drain once more, these gentle giants found that they were not built for another kind of life.

Even if they could have gotten along on drier land and on a diet of different plants, they would have needed deep water as their defense against *Allosaurus*. So we do not find fossil remains of *Brontosaurus, Diplodocus* or *Brachiosaurus* in rock layers formed late in the Mesozoic Era.

Brachiosaurus

Diplodocus (dih-PLOD-uh-kuss)

Diplodocus got his name from the two Greek words meaning "double beam." One look at him will tell you why. He had a body with two long beams extending fore and aft. Nor is it very easy to tell which beam had the brain.

This dinosaur had an extremely small head, and scientists marvel that the tiny mouth and narrow neck permitted him to get enough food down to feed his 87½-foot length.

Like his close relative, *Brontosaurus, Diplodocus* must have spent most of his time in the water, munching on the soft green plants that grew there.

If *Allosaurus* threatened on the shore, *Diplodocus* could retreat to the very deep water. There his heavy legs acted like weighted divers' boots and gave him a firm footing. His long neck and tiny head, with eyes and nostrils placed well up on top, acted like a periscope.

Munching peacefully, this bird-brained dinosaur had managed the neat trick of making 25 tons nearly invisible. Although he did not have much intelligence, he was well enough suited to his world to survive for millions of years.

Diplodocus

Camptosaurus

Camptosaurus (kamp-tuh-SOR-us)

This dinosaur's name means "bent" or "flexible lizard." Since he walked either on two feet or on four, his skeleton was more flexible in order to allow him his choice. He, too, was one of the first of the bird-hipped dinosaurs, and was more advanced than his giant lizard-hipped neighbors. *Camptosaurus* was the beginning of a long line of new dinosaurs. He was not specialized yet and there was nothing especially outstanding about him, but he was developing.

Camptosaurus ate plants. He had the nutcracker jaws of all his bird-hipped family. His legs were heavier and shorter, since he was never built to hunt and chase other animals. His skull was long and flat, and there was a horny beak at the front of his mouth for nipping off plants. His teeth were set far back, and this was the design we shall see in all the later bird-hipped dinosaurs.

When he was walking slowly or feeding, *Camptosaurus* probably stood on four feet, though his normal posture was more nearly upright. Then he balanced on his longer hind legs and his tail.

Fossil skeletons of *Camptosaurus* have been found ranging in size from 7 feet to 17 feet. Having neither speed, nor armor, nor the ability to duck into the nearest lake when *Allosaurus* was around, *Camptosaurus* made many a fine meal for the terrible hunter. But his descendants in the Cretaceous period developed a defense against the hunting beasts, as we shall see.

Stegosaurus (steg-uh-SOR-us)

The "cover-lizard" was covered with armor and horny plates, hence his name. If ever there was a walking tank, it was *Stegosaurus!* But he was not a tank armed for attack. *Stegosaurus* did not go around mowing other creatures down, in spite of his fearsome appearance.

What had happened was this: *Stegosaurus* was one of the very first of the bird-hipped dinosaurs to appear on the earth. He had obviously once been a two-legged animal who had dropped down on all fours, but his front legs were so short that he was forced to carry his little head close to the ground while his hips were way up high.

This posture was fine for nibbling at low-growing plants. But it was impossible for a quick getaway in case of attack, so slow-moving *Stegosaurus* grew two long rows of heavy bony plates that reached from the base of his small skull almost to the tip of his tail. Four cruel spikes sprouted near the tip of his tail. An enemy receiving a blow from it would quickly get the point! *Stegosaurus* just wanted to be left alone to browse peacefully among the plants.

This early bird-hipped dinosaur lived during the Jurassic period. He was a neighbor of *Allosaurus, Brontosaurus* and the other lizard-hipped dinosaurs you have met in this book. But he was a neighbor whose look clearly said, "Don't touch me!"

If his armor and spikes weren't able to protect him, *Stegosaurus* was out of luck. He was not only painfully slow-moving, but he must have been hopelessly slow-witted, too, for he had one of the smallest brains on record. It was about the size of a walnut, capable of little more than to direct his jaws in their chewing and grinding movements. The much larger swelling of his spine near the hips is where *Stegosaurus* had a second "brain." This "brain" or nerve center controlled his tail and hind legs.

In spite of his small brain and clumsy build, *Stegosaurus* was in another way more advanced than his lizard-hipped relatives. Their jaws opened and closed with a scissors movement so that the upper and lower teeth slid past each other. This was fine for cutting and tearing meat, and originally the lizard-hipped dinosaurs were all meat-eaters, but the scissors jaws were not so useful to the plant-eaters of the family. They were forced to swallow whole the plants and leaves which they bit off, which was probably the reason they ate softer water plants.

But the bird-hipped dinosaurs, like *Stegosaurus*, were all plant-eaters from the very first. And their jaws clamped shut more like a nutcracker. This enabled them to break off plants and then grind or crush them with their teeth. They could manage a diet of tougher plants that grew up on higher land.

46

Stegosaurus

THE FINAL AGE OF DINOSAURS

The Longest Summer Ends

Imagine, if you can, a world-wide summer that lasted for nearly 130 million years! The whole earth was green and warm and lazy. Cold-blooded reptiles basked in this ideal climate and ruled on land, in the sea, and had even begun to take to the air.

The third great period of the Era of Middle Life, or Mesozoic Era, was like a brilliant Indian summer that went on for 70 million years. New trees and plants appeared, and for the first time the earth burst into flower. In this period, called the Cretaceous, we would have recognized some of our modern plants. Poplar trees, oaks, willows, as well as palms and ferns of earlier times grew on the land.

But the important new change was the beginning of flowering plants. Suddenly there was color in the landscape. Magnolias and laurels and dogwood made splashes of red and pink and lavender in among the everlasting green. The first bees were at work, and they and the flowering plants were to outlast the giant dinosaurs who would die out at the end of the Cretaceous period.

The new dinosaurs at the beginning of the Cretaceous period continued to develop, as all living things must. The giants of the Jurassic period had died out. To develop size alone was not enough. But this last period of dinosaur life was filled with odd experiments, and some of the weirdest-looking creatures ever to walk the earth lived at this time.

Trachodon (TRAK-uh-don)

Trachodon means "rough-toothed," and this name comes from the four rows of 2,000 grinding teeth that was one of the unusual features of this animal. But another nickname for this fellow and his relatives is "duck-billed dinosaur."

The duck-bills were descended from *Camptosaurus. Trachodon* looked very much like his ancestor, except that he was larger, his skull had flattened and spread into a broad bill, and his feet had become webbed.

These dinosaurs evidently spent most of their time in the water. Their stout tails and webbed feet would have been helpful in swimming, and their shovel-shaped bills were excellent for rooting about in shallow marshes and muddy bottoms.

In spite of the fact that *Trachodon* had a mouthful of 2,000 teeth, they did him no good as weapons against his great enemy, *Tyrannosaurus rex* (ty-ran-uh-SOR-us rex). *Trachodon* was a peaceful plant-eater, and his teeth were millstones rather than daggers.

Trachodon was one of the earliest prehistoric monsters whose skin was preserved. Several of the beasts had died and were mummified before being buried. So casts of their skins were left in the fossil rock. That is how we know that they had no armor, but were scaly, and had webbed feet.

A trachodont was the first dinosaur to be discovered in the United States. It was his bones, you will remember, that were found near Philadelphia. And it was Dr. Joseph Leidy who had to track down the trachodont dinosaur's 2,000 teeth and other missing parts that were being kept as souvenirs by people living in the neighborhood.

Other duck-billed dinosaurs grew freakish bony crests on their skulls. These seemed to be air chambers, or snorkels, connected with their breathing passages, which enabled these water-loving dinosaurs to stay under water for some time while feeding.

But as the plant life of the Mesozoic Era began to change and modern plants increased, the duck-bills were not able to change their feeding habits. The peculiar crests and domes and spikes they had developed were of no use to them in changing over to other types of food. So these creatures died out by the end of the Cretaceous period.

Trachodon

Ankylosaurus (an-kil-uh-SOR-us)

This "curved lizard" got his name because of the way his ribs curved heavily over his back. *Ankylosaurus* was the walking tank of his time, just as *Stegosaurus* had been in the Jurassic period. This bird-hipped dinosaur did not have to live near the water as his other relatives did. He could travel safely over the land, knowing that *Tyrannosaurus* or the other meat-eaters could never get at *his* meat. It was locked in bone!

This dinosaur's back was covered with overlapping bony plates, protecting him much as a shell covers a turtle. Long spikes poked out at either side of his body, protecting his short legs. His skull was large and had an extra layer of bony plates which served as a helmet.

Even *Ankylosaurus'* tail was covered with rings of bone, and its end was a lumpy club of bone. Any hopeful meat-eater who tried to get at this dinosaur must have been discouraged quickly with one smack of that heavy tail.

These dinosaurs were able to exist on the upland plains, safe from their enemies, when the water-loving dinosaurs were finding conditions more and more difficult. But the changing conditions on the earth finally were more than *Ankylosaurus* could adapt to, and his kind died out, also.

Ankylosaurus

Protoceratops (proh-toh-SER-uh-tops)

The scientist who named this strange little dinosaur put together three Greek words that mean "first horn-face." *Protoceratops* was the first of a large family of horn-faced dinosaurs, but he himself had not yet developed horns, so his name is not strictly accurate.

This ugly fellow and his family were the last of the bird-hipped dinosaurs to appear. There were some odd-looking forms in this group. All of them were plant-eaters, but their enormous heads were armored, and they were able to fight to protect themselves.

They came into the dinosaurs' world when the long summer was nearly ended, so that their history was not as long as some of the others'. But they were a successful dinosaur family, and one of the last to die out.

Protoceratops was the first and the smallest of the family. He was only about five or six feet long, and he walked on four squatty legs, close to the ground. His head was his most remarkable feature. Attached to a lizard-like body was a heavy, deep skull. It began with a beak like a parrot's, humped up near the nose, and then flared back over neck and shoulders in a huge collar or frill.

That hump would become a horn in later members of the family. And the bony frill would become even larger and spiked as *Protoceratops'* grandchildren developed in their strange ways.

Scientists have found out more about *Protoceratops* than about most other dinosaurs discovered. In the 1920's an expedition to the Gobi Desert in Mongolia made a lucky find. There, in a hollow of red sandstone, was a nest of dinosaur eggs, the first ever to be dug up! They looked rather like turtle eggs, and an X-ray examination of the eggs showed that two of them each contained a tiny unhatched *Protoceratops*.

This was the first clue scientists had about how young dinosaurs were born. In that same desert, so many skeletons of this dinosaur were found — ranging from very young to full-grown older ones — that the growth of an individual dinosaur can now be studied.

The new-hatched Horn-Face had no bony frill on his small skull. But as he grew larger, the frill began to develop. The full-grown *Protoceratops* finally had a well-protected neck. Since this was a favorite spot for meat-eating animals to attack their victims, the bony frill was certainly a useful ornament.

And in an age when *Tyrannosaurus rex* and other terrible meat-eating animals stalked the land in search of food, it is not surprising to find that the grandchildren of *Protoceratops* improved on their defenses.

Triceratops (try-SER-uh-tops)

"Three-horned face" really describes this great ugly beast. He was the last of the horned dinosaurs, and a powerful fighter.

Triceratops was sometimes nearly 30 feet long. His legs were heavy and strong, with the hind legs longer than the front ones. And he stood about eight feet high at the hips. But his head was the thing to strike fear — and a punishing wound or two — into his enemies.

Three-Horns' head was almost one-third the length of his body. The frill flared up over neck and shoulders like a curved shield of bone. Jutting out from this shield were long pointed horns that grew straight out from above the eyes. A smaller, stouter horn grew above the nose. Below that was the typical parrot beak of the horn-faced dinosaurs.

Though Three-Horns ate plants, he was far from a gentle animal. Nature had given him wonderful fighting equipment, and he did not hesitate to use it. Some of his fossil bones show so many scars that it is plain to see this was an animal who lived to fight another day.

Triceratops must have had a vicious charge, rather like our present-day rhinoceros. His neck muscles were powerful, his body and legs massive. When he matched his swordlike horns against the dagger teeth of *Tyrannosaurus,* it must have been a championship match that shook the earth!

Triceratops

Iguanodon (ih-GWAN-uh-don)

This dinosaur got his name from a combination of words meaning "iguana lizard" and "tooth." That was because the man who found the first large fossil teeth thought they were like the teeth of our modern iguanas.

Iguanodon was a near relative of *Camptosaurus,* but he was twice as big. And he had developed a short spikey bone at the tip of his thumb which was probably a very useful weapon. Although *Iguanodon* may not have been a remarkable dinosaur in his time, he has made history in ours, for he was the first dinosaur to be described scientifically.

Back in 1822, before the word "dinosaur" had even been invented, Dr. Gideon Mantell, the British physician and scientist, and his wife were out fossil-hunting. They were examining a layer of rock in Sussex, which they knew had been formed in the Cretaceous period.

Mrs. Mantell picked up some stones in the quarry and, after looking at them carefully, the Mantells decided they were some sort of large fossilized teeth. But whose? Several scientists studied them, and finally they were sent to the great French scientist, Baron Cuvier, about whom we read earlier.

Cuvier, who had been right so many times, decided that these were early rhinoceros teeth. You must remember that no dinosaur had ever been described before, so these teeth represented unknown territory.

Dr. Mantell did not accept the great Cuvier's guess. He went back to the rock quarry and poked around some more until he found a few big bones. Again they were carefully studied. Again Baron Cuvier made a bold guess — an ancient hippopotamus, perhaps? But Dr. Mantell decided to strike out into the unknown instead of falling back on creatures already known.

"This is a new kind of giant reptile," he decided. "And its teeth, though larger, are very like the teeth of our iguanas. I shall call it *Iguanodon*."

And that's how the first of the prehistoric giant reptiles came to be named. Later an entire herd of these great beasts was found in a Belgian coal mine. They had evidently followed their leader into a deep crack in the rock and had all been buried there, millions of years before.

As a result of finding so many perfect skeletons, scientists got a very accurate idea of how *Iguanodon* looked. They knew he was 30 feet long, and had a thick body with a heavy tail and neck. They knew he walked on two feet, not on four as Dr. Mantell had at first supposed. And they knew that the pointed bone which, at first, had been thought to be a beak was really a peculiar sharp "thumb."

Dr. Mantell became so famous for his pioneer discovery of a prehistoric animal that, when he died, a brass plate was nailed to the door of his house. It read: "He discovered the *Iguanodon*."

Some years ago, in a Utah coal mine, the miners working far below the earth's surface came upon some mysterious footprints. They had dug out the coal from one of the tunnels, and they noticed that the roof of the tunnel was studded with sandstone footprints in rounded relief.

Iguanodon

The molds of three-toed feet overhead, looking like giant bird tracks, were each 44 inches long and 32 inches wide. And the distance between each huge step was 15 feet long. How did they get there, and what were they?

Then scientists came to study the marvel. They were soon able to solve the mystery of how the footprints got there in such an odd way.

At one time, the ground was covered with decaying vegetation in a swampy place. This spongy peat held footprints the way mud does. When a great beast came thumping along, his feet left deep impressions in the moist peat. Sand either drifted or was blown into these three-toed holes. Over millions of years the peat turned to coal and the sand to sandstone, as many more layers of matter piled up above them.

Now the miners had dug away the coal, leaving the sandstone fillings in the shape of the giant footprints. But "Giant what?" was the next question.

After careful study and from clues in the footprints, the scientists decided that this was an *Iguanodon*-like dinosaur. It was a kangaroo-shaped plant-eater, much larger but similar to the *Iguanodon* of Belgium and England. As for its size — well, if *Tyrannosaurus rex* had a stride of nine feet and stood 19 feet tall, then this mystery dinosaur with a 15-foot stride must have stood nearly 35 feet tall!

Other than the ceiling footprints, no bones or fossil traces have been found thus far. But other footprints have turned up in mines in Colorado. Some day a modern American Dr. Mantell will undoubtedly discover the giant American *Iguanodon* who, like Cinderella, is known to us only by the size of its foot.

Tyrannosaurus rex (ty-ran-uh-SOR-us rex)

"King of the Tyrant Lizards" was the name given to the greatest and fiercest meat-eating animal that has ever walked the land. Lions and tigers are as gentle as pussycats in contrast to this reptilian machine of destruction.

Tyrannosaurus was a lizard-hipped dinosaur. He followed the general plan of his grandfather, *Allosaurus*. But the terror of the Jurassic period was smaller and not as fully developed for hunting and killing as this cruel king of the Cretaceous period.

When you see *Tyrannosaurus,* you understand why the other dinosaurs of this period who were able to survive had developed strange armor or grown queer snorkels that would permit them to hide out in the deepest water. This monster, striding across the flowering earth on two powerful legs, meant death and destruction to all other creatures. But he himself feared no one.

The Tyrant King was 47 feet long, and he was 19 feet high when he walked among his subjects. His hind legs were massive and clawed, and he had a heavy tail with which he kept his balance. His little arms had become so tiny that they just dangled uselessly. There were only two small claws on each "hand," and they were too weak to help him hold his food and too short to reach his mouth.

This was evidently a creature of such greed and appetite that he didn't even eat with his hands! *Tyrannosaurus* simply snapped at his food with his mouth, destroying and devouring with that one mighty weapon.

Never was there a skull built to attack and feed on other giants as effectively as *Tyrannosaurus'!* In the first place, that skull itself was over four feet long! The powerful jaws were hinged so they could gape wide open. And the jaws were armed with curved teeth that had sharp notches, like the blade of a saw. Some of these teeth were six inches long.

Tyrannosaurus could bite through the toughest hide and crunch the most powerful bones. He hunted the smaller meat-eaters and the giant plant-eaters, including the armored ones. There were probably only two of the armored dinosaurs who could occasionally escape those terrible jaws. Let us imagine what one of these prehistoric dramas might have been like as the long summer of the dinosaurs was drawing to a close.

Volcanoes rumble and smoke in the distance, warning of changes that are soon to take place. But the strange monsters who rule the earth know only that there are green plants to be eaten, and living enemies to evade.

They clump through ferns and flowering plants, moving slowly, munching on juicy leaves, basking in the warm air. The world is a fine place for dinosaurs. And then there is a sudden stir. A few of the smaller, swifter two-legged

dinosaurs scurry past, running from something still unseen. A duck-billed fellow pounds by on his heavy hind legs, leaning well forward in an effort to reach the nearby lake quickly.

Triceratops lifts his head slowly, and stops chewing. He, too, decides to move, clumsily, slowly. Only *Ankylosaurus* stays where he is. Safe under his curved armor, he lies low, hoping the danger will pass.

And then the cause of all this stir appears. Crashing through a grove of young oak trees, towering as tall as some of them, his great jaws open and ready, *Tyrannosaurus* strides across the green ground.

His wicked little eyes catch sight of *Ankylosaurus,* and he bounds over toward him, his jaws gaping wider. The Tyrant King's tiny arms are useless, so he lowers his great head and prepares to attack his prey with his teeth.

The huge sharp teeth strike the armored back of the intended victim, but they make no impression on this bony fortress. Instead, *Ankylosaurus* swings his heavy club of a tail. There is a sharp crack as it connects with the Tyrant's tender jaw. A tooth breaks, and the great animal backs off, grunting in pain and rage. This creature is evidently not good to eat!

The little red eyes look for other game, and they glitter as they see *Triceratops* moving heavily behind a dogwood bush. Three giant strides of *Tyrannosaurus'* huge legs and he is almost upon Three-Horns. But Three-Horns knows better than to try to run away. His strong point is not speed.

Triceratops turns to face his towering enemy. There stands *Tyrannosaurus,* more than twice as tall as *Triceratops.* He has dined on many of Three-Horns' relatives. Yet even the Tyrant King can be beaten sometimes by a desperate fighter.

Triceratops thrusts his heavy head forward. His huge bony collar stands up like a shield above his neck and shoulders, but the rest of him is all too easy to attack. The Tyrant King swings his great jaws open and starts to drop down for the attack. But *Triceratops* stands firm on his heavy legs and thrusts forward.

The long, pointed horns find a soft target in the giant's unprotected underside. The earth shakes as the two great bodies clash. *Tyrannosaurus* stabs at Three-Horns' back with his dagger teeth, but he does not get a firm hold. Three-Horns lumbers backward and gets ready to charge again.

There is a hush over the land as the two dinosaurs fight it out. The tall palm trees shudder as the earth shakes beneath them and the palm leaves rattle. But everything else is still. The plants are trampled flat by the heavy feet and tails of these beasts. And they are stained brighter than the flowers where the beasts have bled.

The Tyrant King is badly wounded and his breath comes in gasps. But he cannot turn and run for his life. He is a slave to his hunger and to the instinct that tells him he must get meat in his jaws.

Once again, *Tyrannosaurus* snaps at the backbone of *Triceratops.* Once again, the long teeth cut to the bone. But *Triceratops* makes one more desperate and painful charge. The three horns go deep, and the terrible giant shudders and thrashes as he falls to the ground. *Tyrannosaurus* has fought his last fight.

This is a rare victory for *Triceratops.* Usually *Tyrannosaurus* gets what he goes after. But this day a lucky *Triceratops* limps away from the battlefield. He will carry the scars of his victory for the rest of his life. And millions of years later, his fossil bones in a museum will tell his story to us.

As the plant-eaters began to die out at the end of the Cretaceous period, *Tyrannosaurus* had fewer and fewer animals on whom to feed. And finally, even the mighty king died out, too. His size and strength and remarkable jaws were of no use to him in a world that was changing and where his food supply was slowly disappearing. In the end, the king was no greater than his subjects in a world whose rule has always been: "Change with me — or perish."

Tyrannosaurus rex

REPTILES OF THE SEA AND AIR

The Sea Monsters

During the millions of years that the dinosaurs lorded it over the land, other branches of the reptile family were ruling, too. The Era of Middle Life was known as the Age of Reptiles. While some reptiles, the dinosaurs, ruled the land, there were others who ruled the sea. And finally there was even a group that took to the air.

The sea reptiles developed in an unusual way. As you remember, all reptiles had originally sprung from amphibians who, in turn, had developed from fish. After millions of years of living on land, some of the early reptiles went back to the sea. But this did not mean that they became amphibians again, and then became fish.

The progress of animal life can never go in reverse, like running a movie film backward. It is rolling forward always, even when it seems to be returning to earlier scenes. So the reptiles went back into the sea as reptiles, not as fish.

The legs, which reptiles needed on land, did not turn back into fins which are necessary in water. Instead, the legs became paddles or flippers. They might have looked like fins, but if you study the skeleton of a water reptile, you will see the limblike arrangement of bones in its paddles.

Having learned to breathe air on land, the reptiles could never return to the gills of a fish. They continued to be air-breathers with nostrils and lungs even after they returned to the water.

These sea reptiles grew to great size, and all of them fed on fish. Some of them even came to look like huge fish. Others looked like sea serpents or sea dragons. Still others were early turtles who swam about in the shallow seas, feeding on fish. One of these ancient turtles was over 12 feet long and weighed more than three tons.

Then there were the dinosaurs' first cousins, the great crocodiles. They lived in the swamps and in the broad entrances to rivers. Some of them were over 50 feet long, and they grew fat on a diet of dinosaurs who sloshed around in the water, too slow and dull to escape the crocodiles' snapping jaws. The crocodiles have not changed much over the ages, except to grow smaller. It is not too hard to imagine one of our present-day crocodiles living in the world of monsters of 200 million years ago. They still look and act like prehistoric beasts. As a matter of fact, scientists have studied crocodiles for clues to the behavior of dinosaurs.

Ichthyosaurus (ik-thee-uh-SOR-us)

The "fish-lizard" is none other than Mary Anning's dragon. When twelve-year-old Mary found this odd skeleton in the cliffs near Lyme Regis she had no idea what it was. Even the scientists of her day knew little about the creature. In fact, they studied the skeleton for seven years before naming it. But bit by bit, over the years, they have figured out the story of the reptile who crawled back into the sea and became a large imitation fish.

Mary Anning's dragon was a puzzle to scientists, because only the skeleton was there. And the skeleton looked like a lizard with a long thin tail (which seemed to be broken and bent near the end), a long snout with hundreds of teeth, very large eyes, and two large front paddles, and two tiny rear ones. The scientists tried to reconstruct what the dragon must have looked like. They sketched a shape around its bones, and it turned out to look very much like a lizard.

Then Richard Owen, the scientist who invented the name "dinosaur," became interested. He noticed those large front paddles. "Very like a whale," he thought. But whales have no hind paddles at all. Instead, they have a tremendous tail fin with which they move through the water. Their large front paddles are only for steering.

Richard Owen decided that a creature the size of the ichthyosaur must have developed a tail fin, too. But since fins have no bony structure, they would not show up in a skeleton. This scientific detective figured that the tail fin would have had strong muscles connecting it to the backbone. And bones always have marks to show where muscles were attached to them.

Sure enough, the ichthyosaur bones had such marks. So the long lizard-like tail bone had really had a large fin attached to it. And the fossil backbone had not been broken or bent. It grew down at the end to support the lower fin. Now the ichthyosaur was beginning to look more like a fish.

And then, some years later, another scientist was working on an ichthyosaur skeleton imbedded in a piece of slate. In order to expose the delicate old bones, the slate had to be chipped and peeled off very gently. Needles, engraving tools, even dental drills are used in a process that may take months.

While this scientist was uncovering the skeleton, he accidentally spilled a glass of water on the piece of slate. Imagine his surprise when the water dried unevenly, leaving a dark shape around the bones that looked like a giant fish! There it was, a streamlined beauty, with the long toothy snout, no neck, a submarine-shaped body, a big tail fin, and — most unexpected of all — a sail-shaped fin on top of its back.

That is how, at last, through detective work, lucky accident, and sharp observation, scientists found out what Mary Anning's dragon really looked like. It had been a great puzzle because disguised in the body of a fish there was the skeleton of a reptile who had gone back to sea. No one could have guessed how closely this reptile had gradually imitated a fish's shape directly as a result of living a fish's life.

Later ichthyosaur skeletons showed that the mother hatched her eggs inside her body and the baby ichthyosaurs were born alive. Little by little, the whole remarkable story of this water monster was pried from the rocks.

Ichthyosaurus

Plesiosaurus (plees-ee-uh-SOR-us)

This creature was named "near lizard," and the name has stuck, though it does not give us a very accurate picture of him. At one time, scientists thought that *Plesiosaurus* was a water creature who was developing into a lizard-like reptile. Actually, he too was originally a land reptile who moved back to sea.

One of the largest plesiosaurs was called *Elasmosaurus* (ee-lass-moh-SOR-us) or "plated lizard." You can see him battling with another sea monster, *Tylosaurus* (tie-loh-SOR-us) in this picture.

Plesiosaurs grew as long as 50 feet. One of the early scientists, trying to describe this monstrous beast, said he looked like "a snake strung through a turtle."

While *Ichthyosaurus* swam through the water at great speed, he became as streamlined as a torpedo to suit his way of life. But *Plesiosaurus* paddled around on the surface more slowly. Only his long snakelike neck moved as swiftly as the line on a casting rod. He could snap up a fish many feet away, and he struck like a bolt of lightning. He was fisherman and rowboat all in one! The tiny head on the long neck was spiked with many sharp teeth. There was no danger of a slippery struggling fish slipping out of those jaws once they had closed on it.

The seas were full of monster reptiles who all died out at about the same time, over 70 million years ago. Although from time to time, people claim to have seen a sea serpent, the only ones that have turned up so far have been prehistoric fossils.

Mary Anning continued her fossil-collecting for scientists all her life, and when she was a grownup, she found an excellent fossil of a young *Plesiosaurus*. It was in almost perfect condition, though it was only ten feet long. She sold it to the Duke of Buckingham for about $800, a remarkable price in those days. Mary made her third great discovery when she found the fossil of a flying reptile, the first ever to be discovered in England.

Elasmosaurus

Tylosaurus

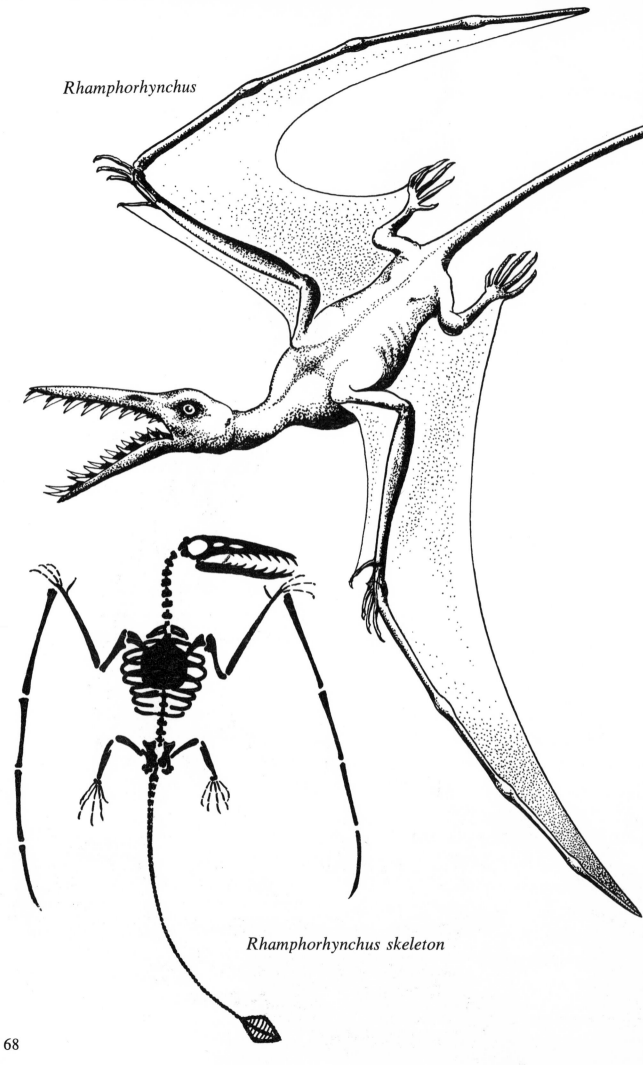

Rhamphorhynchus

Rhamphorhynchus skeleton

68

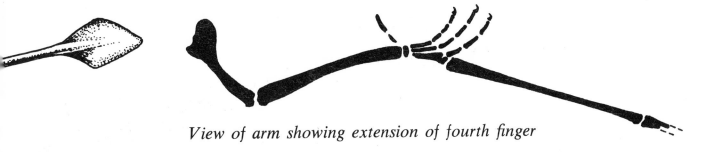

View of arm showing extension of fourth finger

The Flying Dragons

Until the Age of Reptiles, every living animal either swam in the sea or crawled upon the land. There had been flying insects from the time life moved from the water up onto the bare rocks. But no backboned creature had ever defied the law of gravity and lifted itself off the ground in flight.

Then, in the continuous summer of the Jurassic period, the reptiles were thriving and they began to develop in many directions — and one direction was up.

You know that in order for you to jump up high, you need strong muscles, good coordination and good balance. And if you are lightly built, you can probably jump higher, too. It was the same with the reptiles. Some of them developed light hollow bones, which were still very strong. And their muscles, especially those connected to the wings, were powerful.

At first these flying reptiles had what appears to look like a "bat-wing," but it was really a web of skin stretching from one of their "fingers," which had grown very long, down the side of the body. They were called pterodactyls (ter-uh-DAK-tills) or "wing-fingers" for this reason. The other fingers were little hook-shaped claws. Evidently the creature could fold its wings and hang like a bat from rocks or tree limbs when it was resting.

The hind legs were so weak that they were probably useless for walking on the ground. Some scientists think the very first flying reptiles might have climbed trees and lived up in the branches. They developed the weblike wings when they jumped from branch to branch or parachuted to the ground below, much in the anner of our present-day flying squirrels. It was obvious that this early webbed wing would have been good only for gliding flights.

In the beginning, the flying reptiles were only about the size of a sparrow. But they were horrible-looking little creatures with long jaws spiked with teeth, claws on their wings, and a long bony tail with a fin at the end of it.

The flying reptiles of the Cretaceous period had lost their teeth and most of their tail, and had grown to monstrous size. So there were giants on the earth, monsters in the sea, and dragons in the air toward the end of the Age of Reptiles. Perhaps it was just as well for us that they were not able to survive when the world changed and the long summer ended!

Pteranodon (ter-AN-uh-don)

"Toothless-wing" was one of the last of the flying reptiles. As his name tells you, he had lost his teeth. But in their place he had developed a long pointed beak and, to balance it, an almost equally long bony crest at the back of his head.

Pteranodon was the size of a small airplane, with a wingspread of 27 feet. It is no wonder that Indians, coming upon the fossil remains of such a dreadful looking monster, thought it was a supernatural creature with terrible powers.

This flying reptile was probably a glider, too. He spread his great wings and caught the warm air currents, sailing them like a tremendous kite. And as he soared and zoomed, his large eyes were sharply on the lookout for small animals, or fish along the shores of the sea. His legs were practically useless, so *Pteranodon* was seldom on the ground. This might be one reason his kind did not last long.

Pteranodon had a larger brain than most reptiles. Flying makes greater demands than other forms of locomotion. It takes a great degree of coordination, balance and activity. And to hunt from the air takes a keener sense of sight. So the brain became larger in order to meet these demands.

Flying creatures have to be more active than land or water creatures. In order to keep themselves up in the air, they must keep moving. Cold-blooded reptiles are sluggish, slow-moving and inactive, and scientists doubt that flight would have been possible for them. So their guess is that the flying reptiles must have had a warm-blooded system, much like that of birds or mammals.

Archaeopteryx (ar-kee-OP-ter-iks)

This scramble of letters is not as hard to pronounce as it looks. The two Greek words that make up this name mean "ancient feather," and Richard Owen, who invented the word "dinosaur," gave us this one, too.

Pteranodon

Archaeopteryx

While the "bat-winged" flying reptiles were developing, another separate group sprang up from reptile ancestors. These were the true birds. And of the true birds, the first and earliest whose fossil remains we have found is Ancient Feather.

About a hundred years ago a workman in a German quarry stumbled on a strange fossil skeleton. It was in limestone similar to that used by lithographers for printing pictures, and the stone is very sensitive to any impressions made on it.

The British Museum bought the slab of stone with its little skeleton, and Richard Owen studied it. The bones themselves were certainly those of a reptile. But etched in the stone, delicate and sharp, were the impressions of feathers. There could be no mistake about that! There were birds in the Jurassic period, 150 million years ago!

The reptile head had tiny teeth, and the long reptile tail was there, too. But the tail was edged with feathers. Although *Archaeopteryx* still had claws on his wings, the feathered wings were a great improvement over the flying reptiles' "bat-wing."

The flying reptiles died out, but the descendants of Ancient Feather flash across our skies and cheer us with their songs to this day. And the reasons for their survival showed in the slab of lithographer's stone.

First, there were those very important feathers. They had developed as a special form of reptile scales. In *Archaeopteryx,* who was definitely warm-blooded, the feathers served to hold his body heat in, no matter how cold the weather was. That was certainly a better arrangement than the naked scales of the pterodactyls.

Then the feathers made a marvelous wing surface. Instead of the leathery "bat-wing" which, if injured or torn, became useless, the bird-wing was reinforced with long stiff feathers. If a feather was lost or damaged, the wing still worked until a new feather grew back.

Richard Owen's fossil showed another important improvement in the bird-wing. Instead of having a membrane stretched from one long finger, *Archaeopteryx'* wing was formed from the skin which covered the lower part of the arm as well as the finger. Long feathers grew from this skin to form the flying surface. The arm bones gave it greater strength, as you can see just by comparing your own arm with your finger. The other fingers were still claws, but in later birds, those fingers would grow together to make a strong brace for the wing.

Archaeopteryx was no larger than a crow, and he probably was a gliding bird rather than a true flier. But his feathers may well have been as brightly colored as the plumage of the tropical birds we know today. And perhaps he had a strange and ancient song.

At any rate, his descendants developed their bird traits remarkably well.

And we find birds now in every part of the world, some in the skies, some on land like the ostrich, and some in the water like the duck or swan.

But when we see these bright, swift, delicate creatures in flight, let us remember this remarkable fact: the strong hind legs of birds permit them to get around well on land, which is perhaps one reason why they survived when the flying reptiles failed. And those strong bird legs are, in their structure, amazingly like the hind legs of dinosaurs. Birds and dinosaurs had a common ancestor!

The great and powerful dinosaurs have been gone for millions of years. Their little bird relatives are thriving to this day. One group could adapt to a changing world. The other could not. In the long run, size and strength are less important than adaptability.

As the Era of Middle Life drew to a close, the long, long summer ended. Volcanoes rumbled once again, like the roll of drums announcing some great event. The flowering plains were pushed and folded into new mountain ridges. Our Rocky Mountains were born at this time. The warm swampy seas drew back from the rising land, leaving flat dry ground high above water level. The climate grew colder.

Once again Nature had changed her tune. Those who could dance to the new one would continue the dance of life. The rest were out. The Mesozoic Era was ended. The Era of Recent Life, called the Cenozoic, was about to begin.

THE CASE OF THE
DISAPPEARING DINOSAURS

What Happened?

When the Mesozoic or Era of Middle Life drew to a close, a mysterious thing happened. Nearly all of the reptiles that had ruled for 130 million years were wiped out. Not only the dinosaurs, both large and small, but the sea reptiles and flying reptiles as well were erased completely from the list of living animals.

It has been a great mystery to scientists that this should have happened on such a big scale, all over the world, and rather suddenly. For though there were changes on earth, they came about gradually, and other forms of life managed to survive them. Why was it so hard on the ruling reptiles?

Scientists have several possible answers, but they are not completely satisfied that they have found the full explanation.

The Climate Changes Again

The Cenozoic or the Era of Recent Life, which began 70 million years ago, was the early beginning of the earth as we know it. The continents were raised up higher once again, and inland seas retreated. The swampy lowlands gave way to gently rolling uplands. Hardwood trees and new kinds of plants spread across the land. In western America the earth heaved and buckled and a new mountain range was born — the Rockies.

Instead of the whole world being a tropical paradise, parts of it now were cooler and drier, and the temperatures could vary as they do now. The reptiles, who were cold-blooded, probably found changes in temperature to which it was hard to adjust. Certainly the plant-eaters could not change their diets quickly enough to get used to the new kinds of growth. And when they began to die out, the meat-eaters lost their food supply, too. So they soon became extinct also.

The temperature of the seas changed, and that might have affected the water reptiles like the *Plesiosaurus*. But scientists are not satisfied that this alone could account for what one of them called "the time of the great dying."

The Clue of the Egg Robbers

The dinosaurs laid their eggs on the ground in quite unprotected places, and then clumped off and left them to hatch with no further care. This kind of irresponsible parenthood had been going on for 120 million years without any harm to the younger generation. But another theory about why the dinosaurs died out puts the blame on this careless habit.

There were now many small and unimportant mammals on earth living under cover while the giants of the earth ruled. These little mammals had been living by their wits through the long centuries. They were warm-blooded, active, and above all, they had intelligence and cunning.

Some scientists think that these smart little creatures hid in the underbrush, their bright quick eyes on the lookout for unprotected dinosaur eggs. When the earth thundered, and the great beasts thumped by, the mammals cowered under their screen of leaves. Once the giant had passed, the mammals were on the move, aided by their sharp eyes and nose.

The lonely nest was raided, and the dinosaur eggs made a nourishing and safe meal for the smaller creatures. This undoubtedly happened over and over again, but could not have resulted in the utter destruction of the dinosaurs. Nor does this theory explain the extinction at the same time of the sea reptiles, whose young were born alive in the water.

Were the Dinosaurs Sick?

Another possibility is that the dinosaurs' health suffered. The very gland that made giants of them might have also created disturbances inside them. We can only guess at this because we know how that same gland can upset human bodies when it does not work correctly, or when it overworks.

Some scientists have wondered if a disease might have carried the dinosaurs off. It is possible to have a world-wide epidemic of a disease that affects only certain kinds of animals. That would explain why only the reptile rulers were wiped out, while mammals, birds, fishes and insects remained.

But then there were some reptiles who did manage to survive, too. The crocodiles, snakes, lizards and turtles remained through the ages, of all the hundreds of kinds of reptiles that had been on earth. The mystery is not only why did the dinosaurs die out, but why did these few other reptiles survive?

Perhaps the answer to the first mystery was a combination of all these causes. And perhaps, too, the world cannot exist under two groups of rulers. The old must make way for the new.

While the reptile rulers were concentrating on size and strength, do not forget the little warm-blooded mammals living in the background. They were forced to live in all the less desirable places, in order to keep out of the big fellows' way. Some of them learned to live in trees, some learned to live up on the higher, colder land where the reptiles' cold blood would have chilled. And all of them learned to live by their wits, the one gift in which the dinosaurs had been badly short-changed.

Though mammals and reptiles had lived side by side for millions of years, the reptiles had been the chief creatures on earth and the little mammals had played a rather unimportant part in the animal community. Certainly there was no competition between the two groups.

Perhaps in a time when diet, habits and bodies would have to adapt, generation by generation, to the world's gradual changes, the small-brained, large-bodied reptiles couldn't do it. Perhaps it was easier for the large-brained, small-bodied mammals to change their ways little by little to meet the new conditions in the world.

Whatever the reasons, it was not until after the dinosaurs and the reptiles of the air and of the water had died out that the mammals began really to develop in many different ways. And little by little in the long, slow process, mammals filled the places in the animal community that had been held by the great reptiles who were gone.

In the long run, it was the story of David and Goliath, foretold by mammals and dinosaurs. The small, quick, active creature with a brain can outmatch the brawny, slow-witted giant in any age.

THE RETURN OF THE DINOSAURS

Skeleton Zoos

Even the earliest man never saw a dinosaur. He couldn't have, because the great beasts had died out more than 70 million years before man appeared on earth. Yet today, a million years after the first primitive human made his appearance, there are dinosaurs to be seen again by modern man!

How come? Well — and you have probably guessed it by now — we can see dinosaurs in skeleton form in museums all over the world. Many museums are like zoos filled with ancient animals. We can see these towering creatures in lifelike poses. And we can see scientific paintings, in color, of the animals living in their very different long-ago world. This is one of the marvels of modern science.

Our zoos of live animals must depend on big game hunters to go out to the wilds and collect living specimens for them. The museum zoos of ancient animals have their big game hunters, too. And their hunting expeditions are as dangerous and difficult and as fully packed with adventure as any African safari.

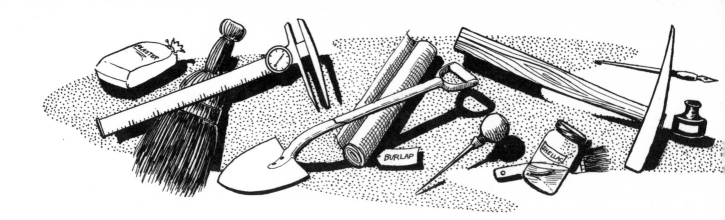

How to Hunt a Dinosaur

Today, the dinosaur hunters are men of science. They know what they are looking for and they have a fairly good idea of where to find it.

The geologists have mapped the rock layers in many parts of the world. The paleontologists know what fossils are to be found in the different layers. They know that the rock layers that were formed in the Mesozoic Era were formed when dinosaurs walked the earth. Therefore, the fossil bones of dinosaurs would be found in those layers, and not in any others.

Of course, not every bit of Mesozoic rock has dinosaur bones in it. There had to be special conditions when the animal died. Before its body could decay, it had to be covered with sand or mud or soft clay or tar. Then, for centuries, the slow process of fossilization had to take place in the creatures' bones.

Finally, the ground in which it lay had to turn to rock. Then, and only then, were the treasured bones safely preserved for future ages.

The dinosaur hunters have found some great fossil "mines" out in the Western badlands and in the deserts of Mongolia. But "find" is almost too easy a word for what they have done.

A dinosaur hunting expedition goes out into the field with equipment ranging from caterpillar tractors and heavy trucks to whisk brooms and carpenter's awls. The scientist-hunters themselves are in trim for the rugged life.

They camp out in tents, endure blazing sun, sandstorms, violent rains, desert winds and pesky insects. These men have to be as hardy as mountain goats to scrabble up rocky cliffs and down steep ravines. And all the while their trained scientists' eyes are on the lookout for a telltale piece of bone that may be exposed in the rock.

Fortunately, the hunters have helpful scouts in the wind, the rain and the weather. Through the centuries, these forces of nature have beat against the rock, nibbling it away little by little, year by year. That is why, in the badlands, where the harsh land is carved into jagged hills, fossils are most likely to be found. Their protecting rock has been worn away. And once again, after 70 million years, the old dinosaurs see the light of day.

Bring 'Em Back Alive!

Once the dinosaur hunter has discovered a piece of fossil bone, his work has just begun. It is no easy matter to loosen the fragile old bone from its 70-million-year-old bed of rock. Just as the big game hunter must be careful to trap his animal and get it home without injury, so the dinosaur hunter must handle his precious creature with care.

If there is a great deal of rock lying on top of the fossil, it must be blasted with dynamite, hacked away with pickaxes, and removed in trucks. When the fossil hunter gets down to the rock just above the precious bones, he begins to go easy. He uses a pick carefully, and keeps removing the loose rock and dust, sometimes with a whisk broom! When he gets down to the very bone, a hammer and awl are used. Gently, gently, the bone is uncovered. A small whisk broom is used to brush away any sand or rock chips.

As each bit of bone is exposed to air, it is shellacked at once to protect the delicate surface. Layer after layer of shellac is dabbed on the fossil, and then the bone is covered with tissue paper. If this were not done, the dinosaur hunter would have only a handful of dust to show for all his trouble. The age-old fossils would crumble away when exposed to air.

Whenever possible, the scientists remove the bones from the rock right in the field. After the shellac and tissue paper have hardened, the bones are bandaged in strips of burlap cloth that have been dipped in plaster of Paris. Some clever scientist figured out that a plaster of Paris cast, such as a doctor uses to protect broken bones, would do the trick for fossil bones, too.

Sometimes a whole big block of rock with the bones partly dug out is encased in a plaster cast. Then it is carefully hoisted by a pulley attached to a motor.

Every hunting expedition comes equipped with heavy wooden crates and straw. They are the "cages" for the captured dinosaurs. The rock and fossils are packed with tender care, for a 300-pound bone or a three-ton block of rock can still be fragile.

Hauling the heavy packed crates out of rough country, where there are frequently no roads, is no easy job either. The expedition that found the *Protoceratops* eggs in the Gobi Desert used a camel caravan to travel over the empty wasteland. In fact, at one time, when their caravan did not show up with extra supplies, they suffered real hardship.

The scientists on that desert expedition had found so many remarkable specimens that they had used up all their plaster and burlap, and there were still more fossils to wrap. The men could not bear to leave these wonderful dinosaur bones behind. They were so enthusiastic that they decided to brave hunger and thirst and sunburn for the sake of their skeleton zoo.

They tore their shirts and trousers into strips for cloth, exposing themselves to the sizzling desert sun. And they used the flour and water from their precious food supplies to make a paste that would harden into protective casts for their fossils.

Luckily, the camels arrived, after having been delayed by a sandstorm, before anything terrible happened. The hunters and their dinosaurs all got home safely.

The next time you go to a dinosaur exhibit in a museum, remember that even though the beasts were a long time dead, they were not easy to capture and bring back for us to see.

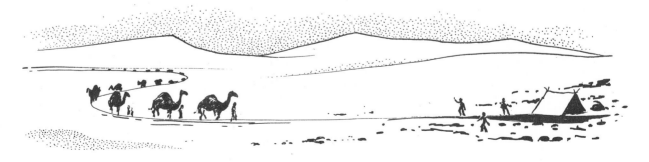

Put Them All Together and They Spell Dinosaur

Meanwhile, back at the museum, crates and packages are arriving as though it were the week before Christmas. And the scientists on the receiving end are just as excited about opening them as children on Christmas morning.

But here, too, they must work slowly and carefully. The heavy casts must be removed without injuring the fossil imprisoned in its hard coating. The layer of tissue paper keeps the cast from sticking to the bone.

Men as skilled as sculptors, diamond cutters, dentists or surgeons then spend weeks or even months easing the fossil bone out of its rock bed. It is protected with more layers of shellac, and cracked places are mended. Missing parts are filled in with colored plaster.

Humpty Dumpty never had a team of paleontologists working over him. All the king's horses and all the king's men couldn't put Humpty together again. But the dinosaurs have had a better time of it.

The scientists have studied so many other animals, both fossil and modern, that they are able to tell pretty well where each bone goes. And, frequently, the bones are numbered when they are first dug up, as a clue to their arrangement.

It may take years, but the scientists finally get the big fellows on their feet once more. Braced with metal rods and pegs and screws, their bones darkened with age, the giant rulers of the earth stand again.

When we visit them and stare up at these monsters who have reappeared after being buried so long in the rock, we marvel twice. One miracle is that such amazing giants ever roamed the earth. The second miracle is that man has been able to bring them back again.

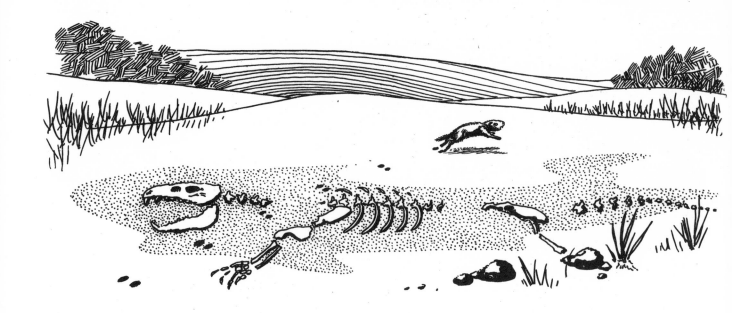

THE MAMMALS INHERIT THE EARTH

The Dawn of Recent Life

When the last great dinosaur lay down to die, too sluggish in the cool air to hunt for food or to travel to a warmer place, a new era in the earth's history began. This was the Cenozoic Era, the Era of Recent Life, and we are in its 70 millionth year now.

Sand blew over the dinosaur carcasses and buried them. Silt and mud drifted down on the sunken bodies of giant sea reptiles. All traces of its reptile rulers were wiped from the surface of the earth.

Then the little rat-sized mammals grew bolder. No longer did they have to climb to high tree branches or hide in holes or cower in the underbrush for safety. They were able to try new foods as they moved more freely over the land.

And these little mammals had three great advantages that the reptiles lacked. First of all, they were warm-blooded and their body temperature was self-regulating — it stayed the same regardless of the heat or cold outdoors. Most of them were furry, and that helped them keep an even temperature.

The second advantage was that the mammal young were born alive. And instead of abandoning their babies, mammals nursed them. The mother fed them milk from her own body, and this gave the baby more than nourishment. During the period that the young lived on the mother's milk, they were protected by her, and perhaps just as important, they were taught by her.

That brings us to the third great advantage that mammals had over any creatures that had gone before them. They were able to be taught and they were able to learn, because they had larger and better brains.

While the great dinosaurs ruled the world, the mammals remained small. There was nothing to be gained in competing with the giants. Instead, the mammals developed speed, alertness and adaptability. They sharpened their senses of sight and smell, and they developed their brains. Thus, the need for survival caused these little creatures to toughen up and prepared them to take over the world when their hour struck.

The earliest mammals were probably mouselike creatures that still laid eggs. The duck-billed platypus of Australia, still very much alive today, is that kind of primitive egg-laying mammal.

Then, there was the group of animals who gave birth to their young before the babies were quite ready to manage on their own. These babies were carried in a pouch until they became more mature. Modern kangaroos and opossums belong to this group. Those mammals are called marsupials.

As a matter of fact, the modern opossum has changed very little in millions of years. Perhaps he has managed to get along through the ages because he is content to eat most anything, live most anywhere, and appears to be in no special hurry to get wherever he decides to go. That seems to be the secret of long, though uninspired, survival.

Last, there was the earliest group of mammals called placentals. They, like most modern mammals, gave birth to fully developed young. Most of these early placentals ate insects and were about the size of the modern shrew. Moles, shrews and hedgehogs are the modern descendants of these creatures.

Opossum

Land of Plenty

There were no dangerous enemies in the mammals' world — at first. The climate, too, was kind to them. Tropical plants that were good for eating were plentiful — fig trees, breadfruits, and nut-bearing trees. The mammals, held back for so long by the dangers of the old world, were suddenly free to multiply and to spread far and wide over the new world.

At the beginning of the Cenozoic Era, many of the mammals were unspecialized, and part of this unspecialized condition was their five-toed feet. Later, as mammals became more specialized, some developed claws and some developed hoofs.

Some of these new mammals liked meat best of all the foods they could eat. Others preferred plants. Over the centuries the meat-eaters developed claws on their five toes. The plant-eaters' feet had five blunt hoofs. In developing to suit their way of life, the two great groups of hunter and hunted chose their weapons — claws for attacking, hoofs for speedy running.

Most important of all, the animal's teeth became suited to its diet. Over many generations, teeth changed and adapted for special kinds of food. Meat-eaters had biting or slashing teeth, while their grinding molars were less developed. Plant-eaters had very effective grinders, but lacked sharp tearing teeth. There was a third group of mammals who ate both kinds of food and had well-developed teeth for both biting and grinding. Scientists can tell with which kind of fossil animal they are dealing by examining its teeth.

In this early time of plenty, there was one group of animals that stayed up in the trees, living on a diet of insects. Originally they were probably similar to the little tree shrews living today. But they developed into small animals who looked like our big-eyed lemurs. This group, called primates, is the one to which lemurs, monkeys, apes, and man himself belong.

By avoiding any great physical specialization, and by improving their brain tremendously, the primates developed into the highest order of animals. Because they lived in the treetops, they had to become very agile. Their grasping hands enabled the primates to do many things besides climbing. Their branch-to-branch traveling demanded especially keen eyesight, with the ability to judge distance and depth. And since they were small and defenseless, the primates had to depend on a superior brain to keep them safe from larger, fiercer creatures.

The primates got their start in the earliest easy-living days of the Era of Recent Life.

Notharctus

Notharctus (nuh-THARK-tus)

Notharctus means "false bear." Though this little animal was only three feet long, including a thin curling tail almost as long as his body, he was originally thought to be an early bear.

Now scientists know he was one of the early primates. He had the pointed nose and large eyes of a lemur. His limbs were fairly long and slim, and he had claws for helping him climb trees.

But it was *Notharctus'* "hands" and feet that showed the special development that would eventually make primates lead all other mammals. The thumbs and big toes could grasp. This ability, which was necessary for an animal who had to cling to branches, became in later apes, and in man himself, the basis of the clever primate hand. When you think how much the human race's progress has depended upon the inquisitive and skillful hand, you will appreciate the importance of little *Notharctus'* grasping paws.

This little creature, whose large eyes were specially helpful to him at night, was wise enough to stay quietly in his treetop during the day when larger mammals were on the prowl. Then, at night, when it was safer and there was less competition, *Notharctus* could help himself freely to his favorite foods. He probably lived on fruits and seeds as well as insects.

Fossil specimens of *Notharctus* have been found in Wyoming. But very few fossil remains of the earliest mammals have come down to us. Their small bones were probably more easily destroyed, and they were less likely to live in or near water or sandy places where their skeletons could have been preserved as fossils.

Most of what scientists know of these long-ago mammals has been figured out from some of their fossilized teeth and a few bones.

Eohippus (ee-oh-HIP-us)

"Dawn horse" is the poetic name scientists have given to this toy-sized creature who began the great day of the horse family. Wouldn't it be wonderful if eohippus lived today? We could have horses for house pets! This animal was only the size of a large cat, though he had a definite horsy look.

The remains of this miniature steed have been found in America, Europe and England. During the period in which he lived, the climate was mild and vegetation flourished. Tropical forests and plants spread richly over the land. Many kinds of mammals fattened on this abundant food supply. Of course, as soon as there are lots of plant-eating animals, that means there is a plentiful supply of food for the meat-eaters, too. So meat-eating mammals became more numerous.

Little eohippus was a timid creature who stayed hidden in the tall bushes or in the friendly forests. It is a reasonable guess that he was camouflaged with spots like a fawn. The spots would look like dappled shade and sunlight in the forest.

But for the times when camouflage was not enough, eohippus had to learn to outrun his hunters. At those times he did not take to his heels. He took to his toes instead. And that is where the wonderful story of the evolution of the horse comes in.

Eohippus had four toes on each of his front feet, and three toes on each of his hind feet. Scientists believe he had a five-toed ancestor whose fossil remains have not yet been found. They believe this because eohippus had the bones of those fifth toes up near his ankle bones.

A later, larger horse than Dawn Horse had only three toes on each foot, and the middle toe was much the largest. A still bigger and more recent horse, after centuries of running on tiptoe, had the three-toed foot, but only the middle toe touched the ground. And our modern horse, the largest and fastest of all, has only one toe on each foot, and he really stands on his toenail. The other toes can be found as little bones hidden under the skin of the modern horse's leg.

Scientists are especially interested in the history of the horse. It shows how an animal has had to change throughout the ages in order to survive. The many-toed foot that was fine for soft ground could not make the necessary speed on the hard ground of grassy plains.

When the world after eohippus changed again, the forests were fewer and farther between, and the plants were not so thick and tall. Instead, there were open grassy plains. Then the horse had to depend more on his size and speed for survival.

Eohippus

Even his teeth changed so that they could chew coarser, tougher grass. Thus, horses have changed and survived down to our time.

For some strange reason, the prehistoric horses who had lived on this continent died out. There were no horses here when this country was discovered, and for many years it was believed that the Spaniards brought the first horses to the New World. But the fossils of eohippus found in Colorado prove that tiny steeds were galloping and prancing across the West 50 million years ago.

Some Other "First Families"

The mammals branched out in so many directions and so many families that it would be impossible to list them all here. Some took to the air, and they were the founding fathers of the bat family.

Others went back to a fishlike life in the water, just as some of the ruling reptiles had done in their day. They became the ancestors of sea cows, walruses, dolphins, seals, porpoises and whales. But these water mammals kept their mammal characteristics, however much they grew to resemble fish. They still are warm-blooded, their young are born alive, and the young are nursed on their mother's milk.

The earth's surface was a more restless place during the Cenozoic Era. The climate changed more often, and new mountain ranges were thrust up to change the shape of the land. But many of the mammals were able to adjust to the changes and adapt themselves to new conditions.

The shrews, moles, hedgehogs and opossums continued from the earliest times. Rats, mice, gophers and rabbits appeared, and their tribes increased.

The cat family and dog family, deer, horses, rhinoceroses, camels, elephants all made their start at this time. Some of their early ancestors barely resembled these animals as we know them now. At first, they were much smaller. Later, some of them became giants. Now just the medium-sized ones have survived.

The Experimental Models

With the cooler, drier climate, new vegetation appeared. In place of lush tropical jungles, there were broad plains and prairies, golden with waving grasses. The mammals moved over these golden plains in great herds, and it was for them a golden age.

But as the animal families which we know today developed, there were some strange experimental models that thrived for a while, then perished. They were like the nightmare beasts of a dream-world, but fossil remains in museums prove that they really existed — some of them right here in this country.

Moropus

Moropus (MOR-uh-pus)

Moropus means "foolish-footed," but this entire animal was foolish looking. He seems to have been a jumble of several kinds of animal put together without rhyme or reason.

As a matter of fact, scientists puzzled over him for years, not certain that they had the correct feet attached to his body. His head and teeth showed him to be a browsing plant-eater, so he should have had hoofs. Instead, each big foot came equipped with three heavy claws.

Then, at last, a full skeleton was found all together out in the West, and it turned out that Foolish Foot had claws, indeed. They were probably used for digging roots.

Moropus looked like a large hairy horse with stout limbs, a short tail, and a long neck. His forelegs were considerably longer than his hind legs, which gave his back a downward slant. As he stood on his big foolish feet, nibbling at leaves from a tree branch, he seemed to be one of Nature's mistakes. *Moropus* lived 25 million years ago. He has left no living animal family to carry on his line, though in his day he had been well-suited for survival.

Alticamelus

Alticamelus (all-tee-kuh-MEE-lus)

"Tall camel" has earned his name. He was 18 feet tall, and looked like a camel who was trying to be a giraffe. He lived 20 million years ago. *Alticamelus* had a small body supported by long stiltlike legs. His slightly curved neck was long and thin. He had two sharp little hoofs on each foot. Since he grazed out on the open plains where there were scattered clusters of trees, he did not need the kind of spreading feet that camels now have for walking on sand.

The camel family is over 50 million years old. The earliest ones were the size of a small dog, with short legs. They have lived all over the world, and it is hard to believe, but herds of them used to travel across Western America about a million years ago.

Alticamelus was an experimental model in an otherwise successful family. One of his relatives, *Procamelus,* was the ancestor of the camels and llamas we know today. *Alticamelus,* with his long neck, was well-equipped for feeding on leaves of tall trees. He has died out, but the descendants of his grazing relatives are flourishing still.

Baluchitherium (buh-LUKE-ee-theer-ee-um)

"The Beast of Baluchistan" (buh-LUKE-is-tan) has a romantic name and an amazing story. He was the largest mammal ever to walk the earth.

He lived in Asia 20 million years ago, and was a member of the rhinoceros family. But this fellow stood over 18 feet tall, and when he stretched his long neck he could reach leaves growing 25 feet high.

Other members of the rhinoceros family grew horns for protection. *Baluchitherium* had no need of horns because of his great size, and no enemy dared attack him. He ate and ate, and grew and grew until, at last, the land where he thrived dried up. His trees disappeared, and he was faced with starvation.

If he could have traveled across country to a better climate, he might have survived. But his great size made it hard to travel. And his meals had to be big enough to match his size, if he were going to live long enough to change his home. He couldn't move, so his branch of the rhinoceros family died out.

The expedition that found the first dinosaur eggs also discovered *Baluchitherium*. The Beast had been named some years before when a few giant bones had been dug up in Baluchistan, India. It seemed to be a rhinoceros.

Then, years later, out in the middle of the Gobi Desert, Roy Chapman Andrews and his expedition made their find. They dug up a head four and one-half feet long, with teeth the size of apples. It was an enormous hornless rhino!

Actually, that huge skull was not all in one piece. It was in 360 pieces! The scientists at the American Museum of Natural History worked for four long months to put the head of *Baluchitherium* together again.

Dr. Andrews and his party found four pillar-like legs standing upright in the ground. Since no animal who dies is buried standing on its feet, this was a puzzle — until they thought of quicksand. The monster had come to drink, but his tremendous weight sank straight down in the treacherous sand, and the Beast was buried right on his feet. The winds and rain and weather for millions of years had worn away the rock and its treasure of fossil bones down to the level of the animal's knees. So only the legs remained.

But the expedition found enough bones belonging to several Beasts to be able to piece together one complete skeleton. Even the tallest scientists could stand underneath the Beast without touching its underside. Although *Baluchitherium* was not able to survive, he was one of the nobler experiments.

The Ice Age Cometh

Mammals roamed all over the earth in rich variety and great numbers. The seas had shrunk, so that bridges of land were exposed between continents. North and South America were connected, and up north between Alaska and Siberia there was another great land bridge.

The mammals of Europe and Asia were able to move over that bridge into the Americas. And the American animals moved westward into Asia and Europe. Herds of horses spread from North America to nearly every other part of the world. Camels moved out of our West down into South America where, over the centuries, they became llamas and alpacas. Some camels traveled the long distance to Asia and even to Africa. Members of the elephant family made the long trek from Egypt to America. The mammals were on the move, and they took over the whole world.

Only in Australia, which remained an island, did the primitive mammals continue to live. None of the newer animals could reach it because of the oceans surrounding that country. So, today, the animal life in Australia is different from that in other parts of the world. It is the only place where we still find certain primitive types of animals now living.

Perhaps the animals were stimulated to travel such great distances by the cooling climate. The ice-caps at the poles were growing larger and they were chilling much of the land. Four times in the next million years the ice at the North Pole was to fan out in thick sheets that slowly moved southward. Those

sheets of ice, called glaciers, ground and rumbled over northern Europe and Asia and down over Canada into parts of the United States.

Four times the glaciers inched their way southward, grinding the land beneath them, rolling great rocks and boulders for hundreds of miles. Four times the glaciers melted and inched their way back north, leaving piles of boulders and scratches on the rocky land to mark its retreat.

With each retreat the earth warmed again, and tropical plants grew where snow had been. Animals and plants alike were forced to become hardy and adaptable to keep up with these changes of diet and climate.

Many died out, but those who could take it are the hardy survivors that live today. The teeming mammal life of ten million years ago is no more. The strange creatures and the giants of each family perished. Mammals are no longer as numerous or as large as they once were.

Primitive man came into his own at about this time. He was able to answer, with his intelligence, the challenges that were too difficult for animals to meet physically. He was able to use his brain in order to help his body.

If the weather grew cold, man did not have to wait centuries to develop a woolly covering. He could figure out how to kill a woolly animal and borrow its coat. The change from a slightly hairy to a warm woolly creature could be made in a few hours by man! He has learned how to speed up adaptation, and he has come a remarkably long way in the short million-year period of his time on earth.

ONE MILLION YEARS AGO

Prehistoric Man Was Here!

From his earliest times, man has had an urge to write on walls. During World War II, walls in Europe, the Far East, and here in the United States, blossomed with the brave legend, "Kilroy was here!" Prehistoric man has left messages on the walls of his caves, too, telling us that he was there. More than that, his wall paintings tell us about the animals that were there with him.

The fossil records that were left in rocks were lucky accidents. But early man left records carved or painted on the rock by intelligent design. If we had no fossils from which to learn, we would still know how the Ice Age mammals looked, for there are accurate pictures of the woolly mammoth, the saber-toothed cat, the woolly rhinoceros and the giant bison. And they agree perfectly with scientists' reconstructions of those animals from the fossil skeletons they have found.

These giant animals have passed from the earth as mysteriously as the dinosaurs. No one knows exactly why. Today, in tropical Africa and Asia, a few of their descendants still live, including elephants and rhinos, to give us some idea of the glory and majesty of the animal kingdom of long ago. But man has had to protect these survivors in game preserves, for even they are on their way out.

Woolly Mammoth (MAM-uth)

The Russians named this animal "mammot," from which our word developed. There must have been thousands of these woolly elephants living during the Ice Age, and because of their warm, long-haired coats they could roam the glacial ice in comfort.

These close relatives of modern elephants came large. Some of them stood 14 feet high at the shoulder, and they had tremendous tusks which curved inward. Sometimes an old bull's tusks curved until they crossed each other, which made them interesting but useless.

These woolly mammoths were well adapted to life in a cold climate. They lived in the open plains, eating grass, and great herds of them roamed about in Florida, Kentucky, California and Nebraska.

They were also numerous in Europe and Asia and Africa. But 10,000 years ago they died out in the mysterious erasing of so many of the great mammals. Now their nearest relatives are the elephants that live in India and Africa today.

Woolly Mammoth

Megatherium (meg-uh-THEER-ee-um)

This giant ground sloth's name means "great beast," and that he was! The hairy giant could rear up on his hind legs and reach leaves from trees and shrubs that were about 20 feet from the ground.

Dull-witted, clumsy and slow-moving, the giant ground sloth *Megatherium* had a very small brain, but he also had his enormous size to protect him. And in case fierce Saber-Tooth came too close, the giant sloth had three hooked claws on each forepaw with which to keep his enemy at a distance. He also had one huge curved claw on each hind foot, and these hind feet were quite powerful.

The single claw was probably useful for digging roots, while the three hooked claws were useful for pulling down a branch of tasty leaves. The giant sloth probably fed sitting on its broad haunches, propped up by its thick tail. It was certainly one of the oddities of its time.

Fossil remains of *Megatherium* have been found in many parts of North America. In fact, President Thomas Jefferson had a sloth bone from Kentucky, and he hoped a live one would be found when the West was explored. But *Megatherium* had died out 10,000 years ago.

There are sloths now living in South America where the family originated. But they are small animals who live in trees and hang upside down, and are perfect examples of why "sloth" means "laziness."

Megatherium

Smilodon

Smilodon (SMY-luh-don)

"Carving-knife tooth" is what *Smilodon* means, but "saber-toothed cat" is the familiar name given to this great killer. His mouth was armed with two tusklike fangs, nine inches long and with jagged surfaces. And he could use those teeth either as sabers or as carving knives!

Smilodon was shorter than our modern lion, but more powerfully built. It is easy to imagine him standing on a high rock waiting to leap down on his prey. His jaws are wide-open — his lower jaw could drop down at a right angle — so that nothing was in the way of those terrible teeth.

A huge furry animal lumbers by and, in a flash, *Smilodon* is upon him. His legs are short and muscular, his shoulders powerful. He can cling to a large animal fighting for its life, and nothing will dislodge him.

Smilodon stabs and slices. The saber teeth are long enough to stab far into the animal's vitals. The animal soon stops struggling, and *Smilodon* carves chunks of meat which he bolts down — his teeth made it impossible for him to chew. Then he stalks away, catlike, to nap in the warm sun, safe in the knowledge that no other animal will dare to disturb him.

Smilodon died out about 8,000 years ago, probably because the large slow animals on whom he preyed were also disappearing.

History in a Tar Pit

Most of what we know about the Ice Age mammals in this country was recorded in indelible black tar. This dark page in the story of prehistoric animals is one of the most fascinating and tragic of their whole history. And how it came to be discovered is a story in itself.

In 1870, on the outskirts of Los Angeles, Major Henry Hancock had a ranch. He called it Rancho La Brea, which is Spanish for "tar ranch." He had cattle and horses on his ranch, but he also had some very strange pools of sticky black tar that oozed up out of the ground. They smelled of oil and gas, and here and there the surface bubbled slowly and formed into large blisters which burst and settled back into the ooze. These tar pools are what gave the ranch its name.

Major Hancock had to be careful to keep his livestock away from these pools. Every so often a young calf or colt foolishly stepped into the sticky black stuff. Then the ranch hands had to rope the animal and pull with all their might to get him free and up on solid land. Sometimes it was too late, and the Major would watch the helpless young beast struggle in the sticky tar, sinking further and further until it disappeared in the black evil-smelling pool.

But the tar had its value, too. The city of Los Angeles needed it for paving its streets. They offered Major Hancock twenty dollars a ton for his asphalt. The only trouble was that the tar was cluttered with bones.

The Major's men spent hours digging bones out of the asphalt. Soon there was a huge pile of them in the yard. To anyone but a trained scientist, the bones of ancient mammals don't look any different from modern ones. Many valuable fossils have been thrown away for that reason. And these bones that came out of the tar were thought to have belonged to cattle, horses, deer, or modern birds.

Then, one day, the Major was startled to see a nine-inch-long curved dagger of a tooth come out of his tar pit. There was not an animal in the world with teeth like that. He sent it to a scientist friend to study.

The scientist saw at once that the big tooth had come from a saber-toothed cat. Saber-toothed cats died out about 8,000 years ago! What other mysteries would be discovered in that sticky black tomb?

The answer to that question was a long time in coming. Thirty years were to pass before the scientist-detective arrived on the scene to solve the mystery of the La Brea Tar Pits. Then Dr. John C. Merriam of the University of California came to the Rancho La Brea with permission to dig.

Hundreds of thousands of bones were dug up out of the asphalt that was over 20 feet deep. As Dr. Merriam and the other scientists cleaned and assembled the darkened skeletons they were amazed. Was this Africa or Los Angeles? Camels, mammoths, mastodons, giant ground sloths, bison, bears, horses, wolves, saber-toothed cats, lionlike cats, coyotes, vultures and falcons appeared in skeleton form from the black depths.

The oil, tar and asphalt had preserved the bones for more than 10,000 years. But there were several things Dr. Merriam noticed that were very puzzling.

As the ancient animal community was freed from its tarry tomb, and as the skeletons took shape, there were thousands of meat-eaters and only a few hundred plant-eating animals. Among the bird skeletons, too, there were vultures and hawks and owls out of all proportion to the other kinds of birds.

The scientists knew that meat-eating animals can never outnumber plant-eaters in a community. Yet, here, that seemed to be exactly what had happened.

Dr. Merriam puzzled over this mystery as the digging went on. He noticed, too, that most of the skeletons turned out to be very young animals or very old ones. And stranger still, an unusual number of them were either crippled or their bones showed the marks of disease. There were saber-toothed cats missing a saber, and with the stump worn down by use. There were wolves and lions with the scars of old fractures on their leg bones, many of them crippled by infection. The mystery deepened.

Then, one evening, as Dr. Merriam was out near the tar pits watching the last of the daylight fade, the answer to the puzzle was acted out before his very eyes. As the light faded, the black pool gleamed like a watery surface. A duck glided down out of the sky, and instantly its feet and wings were mired in the tar. Too late, it realized its mistake. It quacked in terror and tried to flap its wings, but it was stuck like a fly on flypaper.

Little field mice who had been scurrying along the hard edge of the pool in safety were startled and ran out too far onto the soft tar. Their frantic squeaks were added to the duck's as they thrashed around trying to lift their paws out of the gluey blackness.

As Dr. Merriam watched in horrified fascination, the dark silent shapes of two owls sped out of a nearby wood. They had been attracted by the cries of the trapped animals. Without a sound, they dropped to feed on the struggling creatures. And, feeding, they were caught as firmly as their prey.

Remember James Hutton, the early geologist who said that the past history of the world could be explained by what we saw happening now? At this moment, Dr. Merriam was able to explain the terrible past of the tar pits because of what he saw now.

He could understand that, at dusk or after a rain, when a sheet of water covered the surface of tar, the pool might have looked like a fine place to drink. A giant sloth or an imperial mammoth would have lumbered down to the edge of the pool, taken one step too many, and with terrible shrieks and trumpeting alerted the hunters in the neighborhood.

The *Smilodon* and dire wolves (a prehistoric wolf) who lurked around the tar pits waiting for easy hunting were either too old or too crippled or diseased to chase and hunt game on land. They had to take their chances with beasts trapped in the tar. Sometimes, by standing on bodies of other beasts, they could feed and still get back to safe ground.

More often, they were condemned to eat a hearty supper, and die in turn. Then they made a meal for the great vultures and condors waiting impatiently on nearby trees. The birds of prey were often trapped, too. So far, nearly 3,000 of them have been dug up!

No wonder the tar was so thickly clotted with bones! This was a death trap the likes of which had seldom been seen. Young and foolish animals blundered into it. Old and desperate ones were forced by their disabilities to feed from it. One and all, they were lures for the meat-hungry for miles around.

You can get some idea of the activity at this death trap when you know that Dr. Merriam found, in less than four cubic yards of asphalt, 50 dire wolf skulls, 30 *Smilodon* skulls, and many remains of bison, horses, sloths, coyotes, and birds!

One interesting fact has come out. The more intelligent animals are found in fewer numbers. There are many more dire wolves, for example, than there are coyotes. And the dire wolves died out at the end of the Ice Age, while the more intelligent coyotes flourish to this day.

Only one human skeleton was found among the thousands of animals. Dr. Merriam believed it to be just under 10,000 years old. Some very primitive darts and shafts have also been found in the tar with the ancient animals. Evidently, the prehistoric human hunters sometimes tried to take advantage of this natural trap. But they were wiser and more cautious than their animal competitors.

The Tar Pits Today

Major Hancock's ranch is now a park right in the city of Los Angeles. It is landscaped with the kinds of trees and plants that grew there during the Ice Age.

You can go to Hancock Park today, and in the observation pit you can smell the oily fumes and look down on the sticky black tar, where bubbles still blister and burst slowly. You can see part of an excavation, where a mound of solid asphalt rises out of the liquid tar. Exposed on its dark surface is a helter-skelter of 10,000-year-old bones. There, the hunters and the hunted are jumbled together forever.

The dire wolf skull and the hip bones of a giant sloth keep company with a mastodont skull and *Smilodon's* saber-tooth, while a scatter of mammoth ribs, condor wing bones and toothy jaws rest side by side for all time. The lion has lain down with the lamb!

In other small pits located in the park, the age-old tragedy is re-enacted on a small scale. These pits are fenced off behind high wire mesh fences. But an occasional squirrel, insect or small bird still ventures out on the treacherous tar. The ooze holds them fast, and struggle as they might, slowly, slowly, they sink into the bottomless mire.

The tar pits, even as they exist today, form a remarkable bridge back to the prehistoric past. Seeing them, one can begin to think with the geologists that 10,000 years ago is truly just the day before yesterday.

A Mammoth in Deep Freeze

The most exciting bridge to the prehistoric past was the Berozovka (beh-ruh-zov-kuh) Mammoth that was dug out of the Siberian snow in 1901. This was no fossil skeleton, but a whole woolly elephant with hair, flesh, insides, in such a remarkable state of preservation that he might have died only a few days before. The amazing thing was that this animal had died thousands of years ago, and had been perfectly preserved in the perpetual deep freeze of the Siberian climate.

For hundreds of years, the Russians had suspected that there were herds of elephants living in the frozen wastelands of Siberia. Tribesmen from that icy land told fantastic tales of these great creatures who supposedly lived underground, burrowing the snow like giant moles. If the mammoth burrowed to the surface, they said, and saw the light of day, it died.

How did the tribesmen come to this conclusion? Every time they found a mammoth, it was still partly in the frozen ground. And it was dead, they thought, undoubtedly because of its exposure to the light. No one ever saw these animals walking around above ground, so they must have lived underground. And no one could have possibly imagined that the dead mammoths had been dead since the days of the cave men!

The Russian Czar, Peter the Great, had sent expeditions into Siberia to look for elephant herds. Each spring, thousands of ivory tusks were washed down the rivers. In fact, half of all the ivory used in the world has come from the mammoth tusks found by Siberian natives, who then sold them in China and Europe.

Peter the Great was eager to find the source of this ivory wealth. Of course, he never did. But he made it a law that the Czar was to be notified any time a mammoth was found.

Then, one day in 1901, nearly 200 years later, Czar Nicholas was notified. Some dogs had been attracted by a powerful odor near the bank of a stream in Siberia called Berozovka. When local villagers investigated what was attracting their dogs, they were repelled. The smell was terrible! But the villagers could see that the cause of this odor was part of a mammoth sticking up through the frozen ground.

Immediately, they notified the Czar, and he at once sent out an expedition. By the time the expedition reached Berozovka, the village dogs and some wolves had eaten much of the exposed trunk and head. But the rest of the mammoth was frozen solid.

What a scientific find that was! Instead of having to piece together their knowledge of the woolly mammoth from fossil skeletons and prehistoric cave paintings and the habits of living elephants, the scientists now had a frozen animal almost as fresh as if it had died just the day before.

But as soon as they dug the carcass out of the glacial snow in which it had been preserved for thousands of years, it thawed. And when it thawed, the ancient flesh began to decay. The stench of that decaying flesh was almost more than the scientists could bear.

Time after time, they would have given up, but their scientific curiosity was stronger than their discomfort. Besides, they were afraid of what the Czar would do if they abandoned his mammoth!

The great woolly beast was found in a half-sitting position with its right foreleg and pelvis broken. It still had some food in its mouth. Evidently, the mammoth had been feeding on trees and moss during a snowstorm. The soft snow hid a deep ditch, and the heavy animal tumbled down into it, breaking its hip and leg. The mammoth's struggle to get to its feet and out of the ditch only succeeded in loosening tons of snow which fell on it, burying and preserving it in an age-long deep freeze.

When the mammoth's head and trunk had been exposed in a spring thaw, they quickly decayed, and that smell had brought the village dogs and some wolves to feed on it. The scientists cut away the flesh, which looked like horse meat. Dogs ate it greedily, and were none the worse for it.

The skin, with its yellowish under-fur and long brown hair, was preserved. So was the stomach, which held 27 pounds of food — chewed, but not digested! Plant experts examined it and were able to recognize pine, fir, larch, chewed-up pine cones, wild flowers, herbs and moss.

Some of the mammoth's frozen dark blood was kept, too. Scientists tested it and found that the Indian elephant is the mammoth's closest relative living today.

The woolly mammoth, who had traveled so far in the past, made his last trip in ten dog sleds. After a 2,000 mile pull across snowy Siberia, his remains were bundled on the train for St. Petersburg (now Leningrad).

There, in the museum, his skeleton was assembled in a standing position. But taxidermists took his hairy skin and mounted it in the half-sitting pose the woolly mammoth had held through his thousands of years in deep freeze.

The Berozovka Mammoth brings the prehistoric past right into our own times. As we follow the record of life on earth through the hundreds of millions of years of its history, this final page neatly closes the gap between past and present.

Why Look Back?

Today, man is on the brink of conquering outer space. Yet, interest in the prehistoric past has never been greater. Boys and girls are as eager to know more about the dinosaurs as they are about interplanetary rockets.

Strangely enough, there is a kind of connection between the two. That connection is the continuing line of development that started with the first specks of life in the seas and which has led to the first living dog in outer space.

The life of the past may well be a guide to the future. The first fish that left a comfortable life in the sea and dared to explore a life on land, changed and adapted itself over the years in order to survive under new conditions. As a result, life on earth took a giant step forward.

We are about to take another such giant step forward into outer space. Perhaps, over the centuries, we too, may adapt and change. We may become able to breathe air with less oxygen, as the amphibians became able to breathe out of the water.

We may be able to adapt to space conditions without gravity, as the first fish who crawled up on the land adapted to land conditions, unsupported by water and subject to the pull of gravity.

Looking back on the past is a necessary part of driving forward into the future. It is our rear-vision mirror that guides our progress just as surely as does our view through the windshield of the road ahead.

Rhamphorhynchus

Pteranodon

Diplodocus

Ornitholestes